A – I'm an Armourer
B – I'm an Armourer

A – I'm an Armourer
B – I'm an Armourer

The Life, and Loves, of an RAF Armourer

Dave Jackson

91st Entry – Halton

Blenheim Press Limited
St Albans

First published in 2007 by
Blenheim Press Ltd
35 Market Place
St Albans
Herts AL3 5DL

ISBN 978-1-906302-01-6

Typeset by TW Typesetting, Plymouth, Devon
Printed and bound by CPI Antony Rowe, Eastbourne

DEDICATED TO

All past, present and future armourers of the RAF.

Long may they continue the finest traditions of the armourers by seducing
every woman they can and continuing to attempt to drink every drop
of beer that the combined breweries of the world can produce.
(Not necessarily in that order.)

also to

Lord Trenchard, the founder of the RAF who said:

'Without armament, there is no need for an Air Force.'

(He should also have said,
'Without the armourers the Air Force would be a boring flying club.')

**In memory of some of my friends who died
during the time that it took me to write this book.**

Wg Cdr A G (Gerry) Hayes, OBE, RAF(retd)

Sqdn Ldr A (Al) Storey, BSc(Hons), MSc, CEng, FIMinE, MIMechE, RAF

WO Andy Trowbridge, Eng Tech (W)

Flt Sgt Tony Oxby, Eng Tech (W)

Chf Tech Alfie Taylor, L Tech (AR)

CONTENTS

ACKNOWLEDGEMENTS

Dave Andrews
Andy Smith
The Boys at the CSDE

and finally, Mary Ann for letting me write it.

1

LIFE BEFORE THE RAF

My life started during the bad old days of World War II. I was apparently conceived in a field as my parents were lamenting my father's pending posting to the 8th Army out in the desert.

Dad must have had the proverbial twinkle in his eye during those balmy days of September 1941. He had married my future mother only three years before and here he was, about to go off and have a go at Hitler's lot when all he wanted was a quiet life at home. Still, no doubt a few million other fellows wanted nothing more than the same, including some of the evil Krauts.

Anyway, Dad went off to join Monty and the Long Range Desert Group and left me nurturing away with Mum. I was eventually thrust into this evil world, as it certainly was then, in June 1942. I don't think that my mother had a good time with my birth, as soon afterwards she got double pneumonia and had to have a lung removed. Apparently this was a 'first' in the UK as a film was made of the whole operation, and film was a rare commodity in 1943.

The upshot of all this was that I was destined to become an only child as my mother was told that if she had another child she would probably die; not something either my parents or the government wanted, as my mother was a part time nurse. When I realised later on in life how this fact had made me into a shy and introverted little burk, I naturally tended to blame my parents. There comes a time in all teenagers' lives when they tend to blame their parents for just about anything, but I realised, a good few years later on of course, that it was not their fault, and so I felt guilty.

At least as an only child I wasn't spoiled, well, not in my opinion. It was impossible to spoil anyone during those days of rationing. I recall that most foods were rationed except very basics like bread, potatoes and milk. Even so, a lot of foodstuffs that are taken for granted now were just not available 'for love nor money'. I remember that I used to have my daily dose of Health Ministry issued concentrated orange juice and that thick gooey yuk called 'Malt'. My mother was also issued with bottles of cod liver oil for me but I always used to retch on it so she never used to force me to have it. Some of the kids thought about leaving home rather than take that revolting stuff. As well as the free supplies of malt and orange juice, which lasted for a while after the war ended I seem to recall, we had free milk at school, otherwise our diet was sparse. The only time that we had chicken was at Christmas.

All the neighbours who had no children of their own used to give me, or rather they would give to my mother so that she could ration them out to me, their sweet coupons. I recall that the ration was for about two ounces of sweets per person per week. Still, it was a working class community so helping each other out was the norm. The sweet coupons were for real sweets like Pontefract cakes, gob stoppers and aniseed balls. They were always my favourites.

Rich kids had money but there didn't seem to be anything that they could buy with it! I suppose that today, everyone would fall into my category of a rich kid. Imagine telling today's youngsters that they could only have two ounces of sweets per week; I have seen today's 5-year-olds eat that in a single mouthful whilst still in the supermarket before their parents have even paid for them.

My childhood was innocent, like all of my contemporaries.

My first recollection of anything was when this huge great monster of a man with brown skin and lots of funny looking clothes all the same colour came barging into our little terrace house. He stood this long 'wooden' thing in the corner, attacked me for a few seconds and then went over and attacked my mum.

Something stirred within me and I knew that this was not right. I went over to the monster and started to hit him, shouting 'you leave my mummy alone!'

It was dad, home for a few days' leave from the war.

I remember it like it was yesterday, and yet I was just under 2 years old. Odd, now that I am 65 and can't remember what happened the day before yesterday. The 'wooden thing' in the corner by the way was his rifle. Maybe this is what shaped my destiny, as I was later to become a member of that second oldest profession, an Armourer!

Dad eventually came home from the war and life for me was about to take that meandering course of learning that shapes all of us for the rest of our lives; it certainly is the most thought about part of life as one gets older.

One fine and sunny day (all childhood days were fine and sunny when I was at home) when I was round about five, my pal 'Bunnion' told me that girls were different to us, not just because they wore funny clothes, or that they never seemed to have their hair cut, or just because they always wanted to play stupid games, but because of other reasons. I didn't believe him of course. Why should they be any different. I hadn't got any sisters to know about these things anyway.

I told him he was talking a load of old baloney so he took me and his little sister down to the bottom of his garden and stuffed my hand in her knickers. It seemed very odd to discover that they seemed to be lacking in something that I knew all the lads seemed to have. That puzzled me for a number of years; how did they go to the toilet for a wee? Still, now I knew why girls couldn't write their names in the snow by urinating, like all us lads seemed to do. Even so, I got this strange feeling that eventually I would discover why they were so different from us. Only later did I learn that Bunnion's sister, who was a year younger than me, used to regularly go round all the boys proving to them how she was different.

My first school was Thrumpton Lane School, which was about three miles away. It was both an Infants and Junior school. Whilst the school itself was mixed, it was split up into boys' classes and girls' classes. Even at playtime the boys and girls were kept to separate times so that we could not get up to any mischief.

Even so, I 'married' a girl called Sheila Williams when I was only about 9 or 10. We used a brass curtain ring, which I put on whichever finger it fitted and announced to our parents that we were now married. Her nickname was 'Flossy', as she had blonde hair that covered her head in bubbles. I used to think that she was lovely. My interest in the opposite sex had begun. However, I think that she must have 'divorced' me a few days later, or was it that my parents had just bought me a pedal car or something similar and I changed my allegiance to that; I can't quite remember.

We lads used to walk to and from school every day, no matter what the weather. I don't remember any girls in our group, but they probably also walked. Now this route took us for a mile or so down The Great North Road, the A1 from London to Edinburgh. Yes, we walked, and yes, we had to cross this road to get to school. The little cherubs of today all travel to school in mum's car, even if it is just a few hundred yards away; what a sad world we live in today!

All days at school seemed to be cold, both inside and out. In the winter we used to have some great 'slides' in the playground though. A sheet of solid ice that was polished like glass, diagonally across the playground. Leather soled shoes and boots were the order of the day, anyone in 'wellies' or studs was banned from using the slide.

We used to have our school dinners in the assembly room. The dinners were not cooked at the school but were delivered in from somewhere else in great big tin containers. When the dinners were late in arriving, which I recall was quite often, one of the teachers used to insist that I stand on the table and recite a little story that my mother taught me, and her mother before her etc. I don't know why this particular teacher was so enthusiastic but she used to go on about not losing these things out of the local folklore. It went like this (in North Nottinghamshire dialect):

As agh wos gooin t'tree-eckle shop fur earf a pahnd o tre-eckle, agh met me ode pal, Mickey Fumb.
An ee sez t meh, 'argh yer gooin ter feear t'neet?'
Agh fote a bit an agh fote a bit. 'Argh, we mate an all.' So we went.
Eee an it wos good.
An ee sez t meh, 'Sha we goo on't torses nagh?'
Agh fote a bit an agh fote a bit. 'Argh, we mate an all.' So we went.
Ee an it wos good.
An ee sez t meh, 'Sha we goo ooam nagh?'
Agh fote a bit an agh fote a bit. 'Argh, we mate an all.' So we went.
An as agh wos tek-kin me cooat off, a wuman cum t dooer, an she sez t me, 'Are yer gunna see Mickey Fumb, air ee is bad?'
Agh fote a bit an agh fote a bit. 'Argh, agh mate an all. So agh went.
Air an ee wos bad.
An ee sez t meh, 'If agh dee, shall tha cum t foon-a-ral?'
Agh fote a bit an agh fote a bit. 'Argh, agh mate an all.' So agh went.
Ee an it was a foon-a-ral, sum wus rorin, sum wus laffin, but agh fink agh ror'd moo-ast coz it wos my ode pal, Micky Fumb.

That will please my old teacher; written down for posterity. Just in case some of you haven't got a clue what that poem was about, I will give you the first few lines written in the good old Queen's English.

As I was going to the treacle shop, for half a pound of treacle, I met my old pal Mickey Fumb

And he says to me, 'Are you going to the fair tonight?'
I thought a bit and I thought a bit. 'Yes, we might as well.' So we went.
Eee, and it was good.

You get the drift now?

Boyhood was fun! Good, clean and honest (well mostly honest) fun.

We all used to live on the edge of a small market town in Nottinghamshire called East Retford. It was just a small industrial town with a population of about 25,000. It is on the Kings Cross to Edinburgh railway line, with a Grimsby to Sheffield line crossing in the middle of town, so was quite important in its day. There was only one road into our part of town, which was called Newtown. (I never knew why, it certainly wasn't any younger than the rest of the town.)

Newtown had a housing population of about a hundred houses and one big gang of us kids, all boys of course, I haven't a clue what the girls did; I suppose that they all stayed at home helping their mum with the washing or something. Anyway, our gang was one that had fun, not one that has all the nasty connotations of the word of today. It merely meant that it was an association of friends. In our gang were Crib, Zola, Bunnion, Onion, Faroe, Crumb, Floss, Tweety, Splat and a few others that I can't remember the names of. I was Splat. Splat was a TV cartoon character who used to evolve out of a spilt blob of ink into a little rascal; maybe that is why it was my name.

No! I lie.

The thing about Splat was that he always used to turn up out of the blue, seemingly from nowhere. That was me, due in the main to the fact that in our house we always seemed to have our dinner at three o'clock in the afternoon instead of twelve midday like everybody else in the neighbourhood. Consequently, I had to go 'in' in the middle of the afternoon and by the time that I came 'out' again, the gang had moved on to another location. But I always used to find them no matter where they went.

At the other end of Newtown was a railway line with a pedestrian bridge over it leading to another part of town called Dominie Cross. We Newtowners never used to mix with that lot. They used to live in houses that their parents actually owned themselves. Because of this they didn't want anything to do with 'us lot', so naturally, if they didn't want us, we didn't want them. They were truly a strange lot anyway.

Further down from the bridge keeping to our side of the line (that's the railway line, for any of you who are about to go to sleep) was a small muddy path leading down to 'the fields'. Yes, these were the same fields from whence I came, so to speak.

Not all that many years ago, people used to call their offspring after the place where they were conceived. Good job that tradition died out, 'cos I would have been called 'Farmer Brown's first field' instead of David.

Anyway, at the end of the path was a whole row of fields. We all used to play there.

The poor old farmer used to keep his cows on that field but they soon learned to keep away from us when we were around. Even though cows are naturally nosey and always come and look to see what is going on, these cows used to keep away. This was probably because we were always kicking or throwing a ball around and generally tearing around like idiots. Oh what it was to have a built-in supply of never ending energy.

All the fields were surrounded by dykes, which used to dry up in the summer. When it rained, the streams used to fill up with fish so we would all get our fishing nets out to catch a few sticklebacks and tiddlers and the like. Heaven only knows how fish got there when the streams used to dry up like a bone.

We also used to jump over the streams to see who could jump the furthest. It was no fun jumping over dry dykes so we waited until they were full of water, to at least 2 inches deep, which made the whole area into a quagmire. Consequently, all of us used to end up soaked to the skin, covered in mud and happy as larks. All of our mums used to tell us off of course, but what the heck, mum used to clean our clothes and, let's face it lads, that is what we thought mums were for. (And for feeding us, of course.)

I remember that sometimes I had to help my mum with the washing. No machines in those days so it was all done in a washing tub using either a three legged dolly or a copper 'ponch' that looked like a flying saucer. This had a broom handle stuck in it and was pushed up and down in the hot soapy water by hand. The soapy water was of my mother's own brew, using a mixture of soap powders called OMO, PERSIL and OXYDOL. It was my job to operate our 'ponch'. If I was really unlucky, I would have to wind the handle of the wringer as well. Most unjust; but remember we had no girls in my family so there was no point in complaining.

Further on down the fields were ponds, woods, derelict country houses and buildings, fields of corn and fields of other things that we could eat for free. I remember that if corn was chewed for long enough it ended up just like chewing gum. Chewing gum was on ration so this alternative was the best that we could have, it was even better knowing that it was for free.

Anyway, I digress slightly. What I started this section with was what was 'further on down the fields' and I mentioned derelict country houses. I remember we were on the roof of this old country house, messing about as kids do, when 'Ruftie' and 'Crib' noticed that the roof on which we were playing was covered in lead sheeting. Even I knew that lead was a rare commodity in those days. We went back to the house a few days later to discover that all of the lead had mysteriously disappeared. I know whose big brother I suspected of nicking it!

When I was about eight or nine, I was sent into hospital for a good number of weeks with glandular fever, where they seemed to take an armful of blood from me every day. Also, I was not allowed to go to school for almost a year. It was great at the beginning but it soon gets boring when all your mates are at school all day and you're stuck at home. Consequently, at least this is my excuse, I failed my 'Eleven Plus' and subsequently went to a secondary school in Retford: The Sir Frederick Milner Secondary School.

It was a pretty boring life in classes at this school. We particularly hated the maths master, a swine of a man called 'Gunner' Briggs. Maths never was my best subject and this guy had a really mean streak. He would walk around the class, rapping the knuckles of seemingly all and sundry. One particular day he took a dislike to me and took me out in front of the class for the cane; six of the best it was going to be. Anyway, after the first stroke he broke his cane on me (this was on the outstretched hand) and said that as I had broken his cane he would go next door to borrow another master's cane and gave me a further 12 strokes. I was in pain for a few days after that but I could not tell my parents as my dad would have gone to the school to sort him out.

The only good thing about the school was the school play, which I was coerced into taking a female part in. There were more female parts in this play than male parts; someone had a perverted sense of humour as the school was for boys only. It was '1066 And All That'. I took the part of King Henry the Eighth's first wife (Catherine of Aragon) and had to sing a little song;

Catherine was the first to go;
She was divorced as of course you know,
Lucky me to be left alive,
I was divorced then there were five.

I also took a number of other small parts, all female.

Whilst at 'Fred Milner's' I made two pals. One was James Bradshaw who lived on a farm at a small village called Rockley. His parents were loaded, being farmers, and James had a three-track Hornby Dublo model train set. He also had an air rifle, so we used to go off around his dad's fields shooting at anything that had the loose title of 'vermin'. In reality, little was sacred except for some of the birds, which James used to like.

The other pal was Neil Robertson who lived in the middle of Babworth woods just on the edge of town. The woods were a great place for us kids to play in as he lived at the top of a cliff that had a slope to one side which was covered in bracken. At the bottom of the cliff and slope was a lake. We used to make our own 'carts' out of bits of wood and old pram wheels and go hurtling down the slope at a great rate of knots, through the bracken and hopefully stopping before we ended up in the lake. We were not always entirely successful in being able to achieve this and Neil's mum used to dry us off. We also used to spend a lot of time just watching the swans landing and taking off on the water. Fascinating!

One day as we 'explored' the woods we discovered some concrete 'block house ' type buildings that I now know to be Explosive Storage buildings. Some distance from these buildings was an area that had 'slit trenches', and we used to play at 'soldiers'. We had noted that the sides of the trenches were made from the ends of 'tins' that were brown and had handles on. We had tried a few times to pull a tin out so that we could have a look inside, but we were not strong enough.

A few days later we decided to take some 'leverage' to try to pull a tin out. We had a go and the whole side of the tin separated from the rest and we found our feet surrounded by rifle bullets (all wartime .303 stock). We thought this great fun and thought that we would take some to school to impress our classmates. We started to fill our pockets with bullets. Then we thought that we would try and look in some other tins. This we duly did and ended up with hand-grenades and mortar bombs by the ton. Luckily for us they were not primed, but we did not know anything about that sort of thing at the time. So, being brave, albeit rather stupid lads, we started throwing grenades and bombs at trees and generally all over the place.

When we went back to Neil's mum for tea we showed her our 'finds' and told her what we had been doing. I assume that she went a pale sort of colour and started to panic, running round to a neighbour who insisted that we show him our 'den'. I suppose he wanted to steal our new found toys; typical of grown-ups. It turned out to be worse than that, they were all to be given back to the army who came and screened the whole area off and took the lot.

Now, I wonder if I could still find those block-houses?

My teenage years started with me becoming a paperboy. It used to take me about four hours on a Sunday morning to deliver the papers and pick up the paper money. I used to collect about £20 from my customers, not all of whom used to pay me, as most paid at the shop. For my week's labours I was paid the grand total of 12/6d (62.5p). This enabled me to save to buy my first bike, a Raleigh racer.

Teenage time was also the time of the 'Teddy boys'. Drape jackets, drainpipe trousers, boot-lace ties, brothel creeper shoes, fluorescent socks, all topped of with a Tony Curtis haircut with a DA (Duck's Arse) at the back and sideboards down to the chin. What a sight we must have looked to the older generation who were still walking about in 'demob suits' and 'short-back-and-sides'.

I passed the 'Thirteen Plus' exam and went to Technical school. This was at Worksop: The Winifred Portland Secondary Technical School For Boys and Girls. (Did other schools have such long names as the ones in Nottinghamshire?) The most important aspect of this school was that boys and girls were in the same classes. Wonderful! Worksop was ten miles from Retford and we used to travel by train. I remember that I once slammed the train door shut on my mate Peter's fingers. He didn't actually say a lot but went very red in the face.

I didn't try very hard at school because I knew what I wanted to do and I thought that the only people who had to work at school were the ones who didn't know what they wanted to do after they left. What did I need all those silly subjects for, when I knew that I was going to join the RAF and never use that knowledge again.

By now I had joined the Air Training Corps (ATC) but still managed to be just a little bit of a 'Ted'. I could never call myself a proper 'Ted' as I never did get the hang of how to jive. That put me at a disadvantage with the girls but I made up for that in later years. Even so, I had a few conquests whilst at school: Angela Bourne, Janet Green, Janet Brown,

Georgina Wood, Hilary Stones and some others that I can't remember. But it was, in the main, only a kiss and a feel; the girls were mostly innocent virgins in those days.

I remember that I used to go to 'the pictures' with Georgina in the famous Rampton Mental Hospital. Her dad was a warder and during film nights, the families of the warders would be allowed in to watch the film for free. We would pass through loads of doors that were always locked behind us until we got to the cinema. We all used to sit at the front and the inmates at the back. I don't suppose that it happens now as it would be too much of a security risk; especially as they used to change all the locks every two weeks 'cos they reckoned that the inmates had made keys for them after two days.

Janet Brown's dad owned a pub, so that made her a popular girl. Hilary Stones was of the Stones Brewery empire and I sometimes ponder on how different my life would have 'panned out' had I married her. I still managed to lose my virginity at 14, but not to any of the girls mentioned above. I cannot even remember her name or where we were at the time.

Ahhh! I wonder what happened to those girls. Where are they now, what are they doing?

The ATC was great.

We had a band and I used to rattle the old skins whilst the other lot did the hard bit by trying to blow their brains out through cornets. Apart from the band, we used to do a bit of drill, practise leaping off walls as if we were descending by parachute, we went flying in an old Avroe Anson at RAF Lindholme (now a prison) and sometimes, when we went on 'summer camp' we would be flown there in a Lincoln bomber.

If we were very lucky, we would get a trip in a DH Chipmunk two seat aircraft. One of the lads managed to do this and sat in the front seat. After a few minutes the pilot asked him if he would like to take hold of the joystick and the cadet promptly made a grab at it. As he did so he inadvertently pressed the PTT (Press To Transmit) radio button.

Local Air Traffic Control then came on the air asking

'Aircraft transmitting "daga-daga-daga-daga-daga-daga" please identify yourself'.

We also used to shoot the .303 Lee Enfield on the range at Lindholme; the same rifle that my dad plonked in the corner of our house when I was two and the same ammunition that we were playing with 'by the million' in the woods with Neil.

The nearest ATC Unit was 2008 Flt at RAF Bawtry, which was the home of Headquarters 1 Group, Bomber Command. As we lived in Retford, which was ten miles from Bawtry, our CO (a grisly old miner called Bomber Brown) used to get the MT (Mechanical Transport) section to provide a three-tonner to fetch us and take us back. We used to skylark around in the back of the lorry and gave some of the drivers following us on the road a bit of a fright. We had one or two people fall out the back for various reasons, one of them being injured quite badly.

Later on in the ATC I used to go gliding at RAF Kirton Lindsey, learning to be a bird in a Kirby Kadet or a Slingsby. We used to stay in the old blocks for the weekend and be watered and fed by the RAF for free and be taught to glide at the same time. When I was 16 I used to borrow my dad's 250cc BSA C10 motorbike to get to Kirton. I eventually got my 'C' glider pilots licence and the form was signed by Lord Brabazon of Tara, probably using an old quill pen.

I wonder where that licence is; it might be worth a bob or two.

It was the ATC that changed my innocence. I started smoking at 13 and buying 'Spick and Span', a girly magazine that was on a par then with the girly section of *The Times* today (i.e. non existent). Still, when my dad found a copy under the cover of one of his old motorbikes (a 500cc 'Sun' with shaft drive and sidecar) he did the good father bit and gave me a right roasting. No doubt he had a bit of a smile behind my back afterwards.

Or did he; maybe he really did mean it.

I also learned the secret of the dark rings that occurred every month under the eyes of all the girls. It is amazing that to this day, many women do not realise that they get these rings one or two days before they are due to start a period. Boys soon learned these things and kept clear of girls during the time that they were referred to, rather crudely, as being 'on the rags'. Apart from anything else, the girls were always short tempered when in this way, and certainly not up to a bit of the old 'exploratory feel' that was the order of the day for us fellers. We also used to sing a song called 'The TAMPAX song', which is still popular with the rugby club fraternity, but I won't go into that now.

I didn't want to join the RAF as soon as I was born but I recall that it seemed pretty soon after. Like everyone else who wanted to join up I

11

wanted to fly. Only later did I come to realise (probably after I had done the gliding) that only idiots and birds fly and I didn't have the sense to realise then that the people who fly were the very same people who run the Air Force. i.e. Bird brain idiots!

When I came to the conclusion that I was not fit enough to fly (don't ask me why I came to that conclusion, I haven't the foggiest idea) I considered what other options might be available to me. By a method of deduction that only my innermost brain is able to comprehend, I came to the conclusion that I enjoyed playing around with all that ammo that we found in the woods, so an armourer I was to be.

2

RAF HALTON

(The College of Knowledge)

I attended selection interviews at RAF Halton, along with about 1,000 other would-be brats. Halton apprentices had always been called 'Trenchard's brats', as Lord Trenchard had first suggested setting up a specialised technical training college to train the 'high tech' personnel who would be required to maintain modern aircraft.

I was intent on being an armourer even though 'they' tried to get me to be a 'sooty' (Engine Fitter), 'rigger' (Airframe Fitter) or a 'fairy' (Electronics). They eventually realised that I really did want to be a 'Plumber' so I was accepted for training in the Armament trade. As an aside, all trades had their own peculiar nicknames, including 'snow-drops' for the RAF police, because they used to wear a white plastic cover on their peaked hats, which they always wore; 'shine-ies' or 'pencil-pushers' for the administrative folk (shine-ies was because they were always sitting down at a desk and the seats of their trousers always looked shiny); 'sparkies' for the electric trades, both aircraft and ground types. Of course, most people know that the 'brass' were the senior officers; 'zobbits' were any officer, usually the more junior; 'steelies' were our steely eyed killers, i.e. the aircrews (apart from the 'rock-apes' who were the RAF regiment and their job was to kill, but we never used to consider that the 'Rocks' were even part of the Air Force). Even the other services had their own nicknames; the Army lads were called 'pongos' to their faces but 'grunts' behind their backs (being because of their dubious intelligence), and the Navy were 'fish-heads' for obvious reasons. The Navy called both the RAF and army lads 'land-crabs' and the army used to call us 'brylcreams' because they could not think of anything else apart from what their dads had called us in the Second World War.

I reported, along with about 240 other lads of all aircraft trades (except the fairies who did their training at RAF Locking near Weston-Super-Mare, commonly called Weston-Super-Mud due to the lack of sand on the beach), to Wendover station and bussed the few miles to Halton. We were going to be 'The 91 Entry'. We were then divided into three groups to be sent to 1, 2 or 3 Wing.

I went to 3 Wing on 20 January 1959. There were three 'entries' per year and the apprenticeship lasted for three years. Therefore, at any one time there were 9 'entries' at Halton from the most senior entry to us, the most junior, who, like all of our predecessors who had been in that position, were called 'The Rooks'.

Our first duty was the 'Oath of Allegiance'. I joined this long line and muttered some words at the appropriate time, that apparently meant that if I did not do as I was told, I could be shot. Even so, I was still stupid enough to swear allegiance to The Queen, for which I was given the customary 'shilling' (5 new pence). My first pay-day!

Pay-days were a bit odd. We were all paid in cash and had to assemble for pay parade. We started out with the A's, so the Andrewses, Andertons etc. were the first paid (remember that there were 250 of us to be paid). The next week they started with the B's, which meant that the A's were last to be paid. Pay parade, whilst it was a parade and should have meant that all 250 of us should have been present, crammed into a room the size of 20 bed-spaces, took place during the evening meal time. 'They' turned a blind eye to the fact that about 75 percent of the entry just wasn't there, as they were having their tea, i.e. absent from the parade. The whole idea was self-management, to guess the time that we were to be called for pay and arrive from the mess in time to collect it. If we happened to be late it meant either a bollocking from the Flight Sergeant or being put on a charge if it happened more than once.

I remember one of our guys was called Pete Ward. His service number was 685000. Now, when our name was called out to be paid, we had to come to attention and shout out our last three. e.g. 'Sir, 985' (in my case as my number was 684985). However, Pete Ward would often shout out in response to his name being called, 'Sir, zero nothing nought'. He was always getting a bollocking for that but I don't think that they ever charged him for it.

We were issued with all of our 'kit', which included a pint pot, made out of pot and not metal, and a knife, fork and spoon. We had to collect our pot and 'irons' from our barrack rooms before we dashed off to be fed in the mess. At the end of the meal we had to wash our pot and 'irons' in water that was so scalding hot that all that they ever got was a cursory rinse. At least they had been sterilised!

One of my many other surprises, apart from having to live in the same room as 19 other young hopefuls, was that we were going to be back at school for 'Readin, Ritin n Rithmatic'. That really set me back on my heels to think that I was going to have to try and learn all the things that I should have learned at school.

The first six weeks were the usual bull. Learning how to walk together, called 'marching' I believe, in the military style, waving our arms about all at the same time instead of having them stuffed in our pockets. Shaving every day, even though we were only circa 16 and most of us had never shaved at all. Learning how to hang our shirts and jackets in the wardrobe so that only the left arm was showing and all of the hooks of the hangers faced the same way, i.e. open end in first and, of course, learning how to lay out our kit for a kit inspection.

This was a bit harrowing at first as we were not allowed to have any form of civilian clothing whatsoever. This even included things like underpants and vests and the like. As a kit inspection also included a room inspection, hiding our contraband 'shreddies' (underpants, as the issue ones were so uncomfortable) became quite a challenge; we were not allowed to have cars or motorbikes or anything like that on camp, so that avenue was not an option. We mostly hid them in the folds of our blanket pack and hoped that 'they' would not pull our packs apart.

One thing that we quickly learned about inspections was how to hoodwink the inspecting officer. We learned that when we cleaned the windows using that good old fashioned method of newspaper and vinegar, we would leave just a tiny bit with a slight smear on it. Whilst it was obvious that we had cleaned the window, the smear gave the inspecting officer something to complain about and he would not bother too much after that. He used to have a little moan about not having our mums to do things for us and then he would be off, proud in the fact that he had done his job well.

We also had to have our hair cut every week whether we needed to or not. At first, we did not have to pay for this attack upon our person but we had to start paying later on.

We were taught saluting, which meant that everything had to be carried in our left hands to keep the right one at instant readiness to salute. We had to carry our 'irons' and our 'pot pint pot' to the mess for our meals and during the 'fluster' of trying to remember the correct way to salute, viz 'longest way up, shortest way down and only with the right hand' we used to drop the pot and irons quite regularly. It was no problem for the irons but the pot always used to smash into thousands of pieces. No pot, no tea.

One of the most 'comforting' lessons that we learned was associated with 'Hairy Marys'. Hairy Marys were the old wartime battle dress that we wore. We used to think that they were made from horse-hair as they were so rough. When we had itched ourselves for a few days one of the DIs (Drill Instructors) told us what to do. The secret was to turn the uniform inside out and iron, with the hottest iron possible, the insides to singe all the hairs off. Needless to say, it was illegal to do this as it was considered to be defacing the Queen's uniform and shortened the life of it.

Learning how to take orders from everyone who had been in the RAF longer than us, i.e. 'senior' to us, even if it was only a few weeks longer, was not easy to swallow. Being ordered about by people senior to us actually meant being bullied. This was a right claimed especially by the 'Senior' Entry, who guarded this 'right' even to the extent of keeping the 'Penultimate Senior' entry off our backs. The 'Senior' entry were the ones who were in their last term and about to graduate. Even so, anyone who was senior to us was looked upon as a threat. Just one of any of them would 'round up' a whole load of us to have wheelbarrow races for their gratification. If they were not from the 'Senior' entry and were found out, then they in turn would be bullied in some way.

Everyone in the 'Senior' entry had a bull boy from the rooks who had to do all the cleaning for them, including their Friday night task as part of the weekly 'bull' night.

I was 'bull boy' to a trombone player who was also a Corporal Apprentice (we had a rank structure similar to 'man' service but no authority outside of the apprentice organisation) so, as he held that rank, he did not get a 'room job' i.e. a Friday night job for the 'bull' night. However, not only did I have to clean his brass, polish his boots, keep his bed-space clean etc. etc. but also keep his stupid trombone clean and polished as well.

All the entries who were senior to us upheld the right to tip us out of our beds at any time when we were authorised to be in them, i.e. between 2200 hrs and 0600 hrs the following morning. They also used to insist that we remained in our beds so that they could 'do the tip properly'. Strange lot, still, just wait until it was our turn to be Senior entry! We'll get our own back on the Rooks.

I believe that all this was supposed to be good for us as it came under the heading 'character building'; which must have been a misnomer, as the whole idea of the exercise seemed to be to knock all character and individuality out of us to make us all uniform in our uniforms.

We used to wake up, usually to the clatter of a bed falling apart as it was tipped over, to find that every tie, or boot, or some other necessary item of clothing that was going to be worn on parade in the next half hour was missing. Well not exactly missing but re-located. To the middle of the parade square! This meant a frantic dash to recover our bits in readiness for that first parade. You soon learned to mark your name clearly on every piece of kit that you had.

We lost one or two from the entry during that initial six weeks stint. Some of the wimps couldn't take it and got 'mummy' to get them out. Anyone with any hint of the Oedipus complex soon discovered it in those first few days.

I seem to recall that we could get out of the RAF for free in the first six weeks but after that we could only get out by purchase. To buy yourself out used to cost about £180, which was a lot of money bearing in mind that we were only getting paid £1/17/6d (£1.87) a week. My parents could never afford that amount so people who left after the six weeks period either had rich parents or went out on medical grounds.

I remember one who went out on medical grounds; he used to inject air bubbles into his veins and watch the bubbles travel up his arm. 'They' came and took him away and we never saw him again. I think they locked him up for a bit first. Paddy Rye, where are you, are you still alive?

After the first six week period, the next phase of our training consisted of 'school' type subjects like Maths, Mechanics, English, Science and associated studies (RAF history, mostly about the Second World War which, according to the RAF, was won entirely by them; heaven only knows what dad did when he was in the Long Range Desert Group during the war!), and workshop type subjects. Over the three year apprenticeship the ratio averaged out at about 50/50 between schools and workshops.

We had the usual sports afternoon on Wednesdays, but Saturday mornings were for parades and kit inspections etc. The rest of the weekend was our own when we wandered around camp exploring and the like.

School subjects were the usual sort of thing, but now that I realised that the RAF actually wanted me to be just a little bit literate, as well as learning how to hold a hammer at the end of its shaft instead of just by the head, I attacked the subjects with just a bit more interest.

The Workshops phase started off with us spending 14 weeks with a file in our hands. There was this peculiar rule that unless we could file a piece of metal to a 'one thou' precision we could never be classed as a fitter, which meant that we could never graduate as a Technician. We used to steal all the chalk from school and rub it onto the finest of 'smooth' files so that we ended up with a mirror-like finish. (Emery paper and metal polish were banned under pain of having to start the lot again.)

After all that skill gained with a file I don't suppose that I have spent more than an hour in my 38 years service filing metal in the service of The Queen.

After we had successfully completed our 'test piece' with the file we went on to learn in the space of a week for each subject the art of welding, tin-smithing and black-smithing. Only after that did we, the riggers and sooties, start to learn about the nuts and bolts of our individual trades. At last, guns, bombs, rockets, carriers, explosives and those most dangerous of all things, at least to the armourers, ejection seats. In the early years of ejection seats it was reputed that they had killed more armourers than they had saved air-crew.

By now we were learning about the myths and legends of the Rothschild estate. Rumour had it that RAF Halton had been rented out by the Rothschild family to the father of the apprentices (Lord Trenchard) ad infinitum for a peppercorn rent so long as it was used for training the, then new, RAF Apprentices. The Officers' Mess was the original grand house of the estate and in the woods that surrounded the house was a small building with a marble Pentangle in the floor.

We all used to imagine the human sacrifices that were made there when the Rothschild family was making its small, or not so small, fortunes in the early days. We had lively imaginations in those days!

The whole area seemed spooky to say the least. Every building on camp had a tale to tell of people going missing, never to be seen again. All buildings had apparently experienced someone murdered or tortured and because of this were also haunted. It was probably all rumour to ensure that everyone stayed in their beds after 'lights-out' for fear of going missing in the night. Apparently it did not apply to the 'senior' entry, who had some sort of immunity, just like older children who learned that they did not have to be 'good' all the time for Father Christmas to leave them toys at Christmas.

We used to have a Corps of trumpeters and one of them (it was a duty for them) would blow reveille at some ungodly hour in the morning and play the last post at night. This was always the routine during 'term' time but at the end of term on the last night, before we all went off on a few days leave, the whole Corps would turn out and play the last post. They were good too and everyone used to hang out of the windows to listen to them.

After the last post they would then play reveille; it was a touching time and strange as it may seem, made us all feel patriotic.

One of the first 'skives' that I learned about was to join the brass band. It used to get us out of all sorts of parades and inspections and all the other really useful things that apprentices did.

All of the entries used to march from the domestic accommodation to 'schools' or 'workshops', down the hill and over the main road. The main road was the place that 'Joe SWO' (Station Warrant Officer) used to stand and call us out to give us a bollocking because we were not swinging our arms high enough or needed a haircut or some other item that would mean us losing any future war that we entered into. I am sure that he only used to do this sort of thing on the main road that all the civvies were on so that he looked good, or just big, or that he was giving the taxpayer good value for their money.

We used to be relieved when he called someone out from the flight just in front of us, which meant that whilst he was bollocking them he did not look at us.

Needless to say, we all used to speed up then to get past as quickly as possible. The flight behind us would also start pushing us ahead so that they too could get past, everybody hoping that the one who had been extracted from the flight had done something really bad so that he needed a really long, long bollocking.

We did not have raincoats or anything like that issued to us in those days so we were instructed to use the old ground sheet that we always carried. We used to love the rain because when we had that ground sheet draped around our shoulders, then we could all march with our hands in our pockets as no-one could see us. Similarly, the ground sheet did not have a collar so when it rained we used to pull the ground sheet up to our chins to prevent the water running down our necks. This meant that

Joe SWO could not see if we needed a haircut or see that our arms were even swinging never mind that we had them stuffed in our pockets, so he kept away.

It was days like that we would try to sing (more of a murmur really) our apprentice song 'Yellow Ribbon' .

> She wore, she wore, she wore a yellow ribbon,
> She wore it for an apprentice who was far, far away,
> Far away,
> NINETY FIRST [as loud as we dared]
> Far away,
> NINETY FIRST, etc.

Needless to say, if a rookie entry dared to sing their entry number then they were guaranteed to be 'tipped' later that night. It was worth it though, for we were the greatest entry that ever existed. THE NINETY FIRST ENTRY – yahoo!

Anyway, I digress. During the marching from/to schools and work-shops, we were always led by the pipe band. They were a right load of Prima Donnas, and apart from that they were a lot better players than most in the brass band.

The brass band was a bit of an embarrassment really but as I said, it was a good skive. I had rattled the skins in the ATC so thought it a good idea to continue to do it in the 'real airfarce', sorry, Air Force. We sometimes had to play during parades, but not often because we were so bad. Even so, we had to take part in the Lord Mayor's Parade held in London every year. For the three years that I did my apprenticeship I did three Lord Mayor's Parades and it poured down with rain every time. It is impossible to play a drum with a soggy drum-skin (remember that all the drum-skins in those days were made of real pigskin and not the plastic things of today that take no account of the weather) and the 'blow brigade' were cold and wet so the band was even worse than normal.

During practice of the band only one drummer was required as the band practice was inside a small wooden hut and more than one drum was too noisy. So, we drummers used to quietly slip outside and mess about. Easy peasy.

In the second year during the summer, the three middle entries would each go off on summer camp, for a week each. We all went to live under canvas and play at soldier and boy-scout type things.

Climbing the north face of the Eiger, crossing shark infested white water rivers on rafts that we had made ourselves out of oil drums and lengths of tree, marching across the desert for 20 miles and then the snake infested jungle for 20 miles, living on meagre war rations and always careful of an imminent ambush by the Soviet Spetznatz. Not bad for a week in Cornwall.

One day, our little flight was detailed to assist the cooks in making 10 million sandwiches (this figure might be a small exaggeration) and we were detailed to spread margarine on this mountain of bread. As it was very hot, the margarine was soft and runny so we had this idea that we would go and get our shaving brushes and use them to spread the marg. It took us no time at all and the cooks thought that we were super efficient; little did they know!

I must admit that some of the sandwiches tasted a bit peculiar but we made sure that we ate the last that had been made. All the shaving cream was spread on the earlier sandwiches by then and in any case, we packed the inside of 'our' sandwiches full of the best ham.

All of this was during the daylight hours; at night we all used to try to get into Newquay as much as possible, chatting up the tourist girls. Cornwall was very hot that year, and not just the weather!

The entry also organised a holiday to Paris for those who wanted to go. Everybody settled into little groups and Mick Keitch, Ray Binmore, and 'Rangit', from Ceylon (now called Sri Lanka) who was one of the foreigners in our entry, all decided to go.

We used to have all sorts of nationalities in the apprentices. Australians, New Zealanders, Burmese, Indians and Venezualans. The 'Vennies' were reputed to run most of the brothels in London at the time, passing them on to their replacements when they finished their Halton stint. The 'Vennies' always seemed to have loads of money, whether it was because of the brothels or because they were just paid more than us I don't know.

Anyway, we went off to Paris and did all the usual touristy type things. We went to the Crazy Horse Saloon in Avenue George V, which was supposed to be quite famous for its girls. The entertainment consisted of strippers, followed by a non-stripper act then strippers again etc.

Once we had seen a couple of strippers we got bored and talked and drank our beer during the stripper act and started to watch the magician, singer, trumpet player or whatever act was on. We quickly came to the conclusion that one naked female looks much the same as any other naked female, when they all have slim, trim bodies and big boobs. Even the faces looked much the same under all that make-up.

In the last year of our apprenticeship, all of the bullying that had been forced upon us had been wiped out, so we never did get our own back on the rooks. We were not even allowed to tip beds or pinch clothing to put on the parade square or anything.

I think the change came about when one of the senior entries 'borrowed' a drill 1000 lb bomb from workshops, took it down to Wendover Railway station and half buried it in a hole that some workmen had just dug the day before. It closed the whole of the main rail line into London all day long and most of the people of Wendover were evacuated to the safe haven of RAF Halton.

We all thought that it was an absolutely brilliant scam but apparently our lords and masters thought differently. Nothing was ever the same again.

We were allowed to wear 'mufti' in our last year. Mufti was an approved blazer, grey slacks, black shoes and RAF tie. Up until then we were not allowed any civilian clothes at all, travelling everywhere, including to and from home on leave, in 'Best Blue' uniform. Mufti was a great honour for us but could be taken away if we 'showed up' and brought the Air Force into any disrepute.

In the last three months of our apprenticeship we were allowed to wear an approved suit, complete with approved shirt, approved tie and approved shoes. Approval was by our Flight Commanders who inspected us in our suits (or mufti if we did not own a suit) to ensure that they were suitable. If he thought that they were not suitable, they were taken from us and locked away until we next went home on leave so that we could take the offending articles back to mum. Needless to say, with such a strict regime, we were not allowed cars or motorbikes at all.

Some of us used to keep a car or motorbike in the street in Aylesbury during the week and just use them at weekends and leave, or on one of the few nights that we were allowed off camp during the week. Even in the last year we were only allowed off camp for two nights of the week. I used to have a little 100E Ford Anglia with an 1172cc side valve engine that did 60 mph and 30 mpg (no matter how it was driven). Even so, that car made life much better, as we used to go driving around all over the area.

One evening we thought that we would go to see the Luton Girls Choir for a laugh. Some laugh; we all promptly fell madly in lust with quite a few of the girls. We soon spread the word and the choir would be followed by hordes of sex starved young and virile apprentices. There was something there for everyone. After the singing was over was the time for mass orgies. Some of those girls were really randy little tramps and we lost all inhibitions about being 'second' (or even up to sixth) in line to screw one.

Nobody had any inhibitions after those girls.

When we were the senior entry (i.e. during our last 4 months) we were watched by 'them' so much that it was impossible to get up to the tricks that had been imposed upon us. Even that time honoured tradition of tipping beds had been banned. We had an entry meeting and decided that we had to do something, no matter how harmless and innocuous it was. We decided to go 'missing'.

The last phase of our training was 'airfields' where we learned about hangar and servicing bay activities. The airfield was about four miles away and we used to be bussed there in clapped out double-decker buses with pre-select gearboxes. We all decided that we would skip breakfast and creep down the airfield in the dead of night without being seen. Someone had copied the hangar key and all 250 of us made it into the hangar without anyone knowing.

Breakfast was the first time that we were missed. We were not there to catch the bus and it took a while for the 'powers that be' to find out what we had done.

I eventually graduated from Halton with a string of 'O' and 'A' level GCE's and an ONC in Mechanical Engineering (I think that I was one of about 30 odd who got the ONC from my entry).

I was also a 'fitter' with the rank of Junior Technician, which meant that I wore a single stripe (Chevron) upside down. I told my parents that the stripe pointed towards my brain because I was a technician whilst the army wore stripes that pointed to their feet for obvious reasons.

We were all sent for a few days leave and then it was our first posting to the real Air Force.

3

RAF FINNINGLEY

(*The VEE Bomber Force*)

So this was it! The mighty V Bomber force located just outside Doncaster.

I was allocated to a room with only nine other people in it; luxury! I had my little 100E side valve Anglia car so I could go off camp whenever I wanted to and even stay out overnight if I wanted to, or should I say, whenever my luck was in and the opportunity arose. This was one of the great things about 'man service', so long as we were at work at the allotted time, nobody gave a hoot about what you did or where you were in the intervening times. So long as I was at work by 0800 Hours and did not finish until 'round about' 1700 Hours nobody bothered me.

The unit still had some of the last national servicemen around, who were always under-employed. As long as they walked around camp all day long with a spanner and a greasy rag in their hand, no-one would bother them.

Wednesday afternoons were sports afternoon for anyone who wanted to play some sort of sport. Most people used the afternoon to fix the car, go downtown shopping or a hundred and one other things that people can do during the weekday. We used to work one Saturday morning in four to make up the hours lost for the sports afternoon. Not a bad deal really.

My first decision was whether to take my HNC to follow on from the ONC that I had just gained at Halton. As I decided that my ONC was not going to make a jot of a difference to me whilst I was in the RAF, apart from being badgered by my Flt Cmdr to apply for a commission, which I definitely did not want, I decided that I would not bother and have a good time instead.

Most of the guys in the room had their own cars so we all took it in turns to drive. We managed to get out almost every night in either one or two cars. The only reason why we did this was because of the petrol money, nothing to do with drink driving as it didn't really exist in those days so it did not influence the drivers drinking pattern. Consequently, some of those drives back to camp late at night were quite hairy.

I remember Jock used to go over the one roundabout that we encountered, because he could not negotiate around them in his big old Opel Kapitan. His steering was shot and the car was a big old 'tank' anyway and this was in the days before MoT's. I also remember that his door locks were not very good. One night, whilst Jock was fighting to negotiate a bend, the door sprang open and the other Jock, who we used to call Scotty to avoid confusion, was thrown out of the car, rolled over a few times, picked himself up and got back into the car unharmed. If Scotty had been sober he would have probably killed himself or hurt himself badly.

I had got in with a group, all armourers of course, which consisted of two Scots, a Paddy, a Taff and me, the only Englishman. We all used to drink Bass beer, which gave us all terrible wind the next day. As we all worked in the armoury behind locked doors the air was sometimes not pleasant for the others to work in.

The other lads did not seem to be all that enthusiastic about the opposite sex; they only seemed to be interested in beer. Nevertheless, we all did our bit of scoring, mostly one night stands (usually called a 'knee trembler') in the shopfront of some shop in the Doncaster high street.

We, all five of us, booked a holiday together on the Norfolk Broads in a big old boat. We made this pact that we would not have any women or beer on board. Strangely enough we all kept to it but did manage to fall in a few times whilst climbing back on board or generally messing about. I think that the pact probably saved us from some terrible, perhaps fatal experiences.

I actually got engaged to a girl called Ann who lived just outside Doncaster. She had the annoying habit of filling up her bra with talcum powder. I used to get the stuff all over me and I can assure anyone who hasn't tried it that it tastes revolting. She was definitely the 'lay back and think of England' type, but what the heck, I was getting my end away and that is all that mattered to me at the time. Like most guys of my age, my brains were definitely in the end of my dick in those days.

However, the engagement did not last and so I went back to casual sex with girls for a few days at a time or just for the proverbial one-night stand ('knee trembler') and then let them finish with me. It was my proud boast that it was never me that broke off a relationship. I always made sure that I gave them reasons to dump me. I had this strange idea that whilst I had been satisfying my carnal desires with them it seemed unfair to just dump them when I got bored. See, the age of chivalry was not dead!

Work-wise, I started out in the Carrier Bay servicing seven store bomb carriers that held the 1000 lb bombs that the old Vulcan carried when not in the 'nuke' role. The Vulcan carried three of these carriers. i.e, 21 by 1000 lb Bombs. However, nobody ever thought for one moment that the Vulcan would ever carry anything other than the 'nuke'.

I also became a member of a Weapon Load Team loading 'nukes' or 'seven stores', when required, onto the Vulcan and Valiant. Quite an easy job on the Vulcan, as the four-man team were all on the floor beneath the bomb bay of the aircraft so conversation between the team members was easy. We used a hydraulic power pack with its two jacks to raise the nuke carrier (or seven store carrier) which were pre-fitted to the stores, and then lock the carrier to the aircraft. The Valiant was a different ball game. We used to use the Symonds cherry picker truck so that one of the team was outside of the aircraft on its back and operating the hydraulic levers on the truck so that the 'Donkey Dick' type probe passed through from the top of the aircraft, attached to the bomb carrier and lifted the load that way. Weird!

I remember once when we had loaded a 'nuke' onto a BCDU (Bomber Command Development Unit) Valiant and just left it. Most unusual, as we mostly loaded and then down-loaded on the same day. When the boss got the order to down-load via his special green 'scrambler' telephone that he had in his office, we assembled the team and did the job. However, the RAF snowdrops noticed some guys on the outside of the camp perimeter fence with long-range cameras. They turned out to be from the Russian embassy, who apparently knew long before any of us on camp that the 'nuke' was about to be down-loaded.

As a driver I was given an MT driving licence annotated 'Authorised to tow nuclear weapons by means of Tractor Light'. There was no training in those days, we were just given the licence and told to get on with it. Whenever we did a load, it was mostly with drill weapons but sometimes with real ones.

The first that I knew whether the weapon was drill or live was when I went to get it from the SSA (Supplemental Storage Area, sometimes called Special Storage Area). If my tractor and trolley were to be preceded by a RAF Police land-rover then the weapon was real; if I was to be on my Jack Todd then the weapon was drill.

We would load the weapon and later, if it was 'real', a 'performance' called LML (Last Minute Loading) was carried out which entailed inserting the 'heart' into the bomb. This procedure was only to be carried out by SNCOs at about 'take-off plus 8 minutes'. It was a complicated system that entailed special tools and an insertion process akin to getting to the centre of Hampden Court Maze.

The 'heart' and the tool was inserted a stage at a time with rotation of so many degrees this way, so many the other way, push the tool and turn as before and repeat the whole process a number of times. The amount of insertion and angles of rotation were all different so it made LML a harrowing time, especially bearing in mind that if it was done incorrectly the whole system locked and went into its safety mode.

All at 8 minutes prior to take off for the Armageddon scenario. No wonder all of the 'snecks' (SNCOs) were bald or grey.

At the end of the main runway was a large area to one side called the ORP (Operational Readiness Pan). When we had four aircraft sitting on the ORP during exercises or heightened tension, the weapon was locked to the carrier and a safety pin inserted. This was before the days of the electrically operated BRSL (Bomb Release Safety Lock).

This pin was manually removed by the armourer when the tannoy announced 'take-off plus three minutes' at three minutes prior to take-off. This did not necessarily mean that the aircraft was going to take off in three minutes as they virtually never flew with a live 'nuke'; They would sometimes have a roll down the runway, get to the other end and then turn round and trundle back to the ORP again. Anyway, I digress yet again. Going back to the armourer who was to remove the pin, he had to position a pair of steps below the closed bomb bay doors, open a small access door, climb inside the bomb bay, walk forward to pull out the pin, and then back out in the reverse process. This usually took about 2 minutes, by which time the aircraft was starting up. There was a member of the start-up ground-crew who was in radio contact with the air-crew and one of his jobs was to tell the pilot when the armourer had vacated the aircraft.

One day, the pilot had got his signal from Air Traffic Control to go and started to roll forward. This pulled the plug out of the aircraft that connected the start crew to the air-crew. The pilot was far too preoccupied to worry about ground-crew (even then the air-crew had little regard for ground-crew; it is even worse today) and he started to roll on to the runway.

The armourer, who was still inside the bomb bay, had no idea whether this was for real or just an exercise (he knew that the aircraft had a live bomb on board) so he planned for the worst. He removed his belt and strapped himself to the airframe inside the bomb bay.

He recounted later that his thoughts at the time were that he would almost certainly die from cold, lack of oxygen, the aircraft would get shot down anyway, or some other means of death that he had not thought of. No matter what, he thought that he was finished and that by strapping himself into the bomb bay and if the aircraft did manage to get back again then at least 'they' would find him and give him a decent funeral.

Luckily, this was only an exercise and the aircraft rolled to the end of the runway, turned around and came back again.

The armourer's legs were just a little bit wobbly as he climbed out of that bomb bay.

I remember early one Saturday morning, we had a covert call-out. All of our call-outs up to then had been overt with Tannoy's blaring out all over the place. This time the police walked into our room in the barrack block and woke us all up (we were all armourers in our room), saying that we all had to report to work fully dressed. Now that in itself was unusual as an early call-out meant that if we reported to work wearing anything other than pyjamas, great-coat and boots then the management said that we were wasting time by getting dressed.

Anyway, we all got dressed and some of us even washed and shaved. We reported in to the armoury and were constituted into loading teams and started loading live nuclear weapons onto all of the aircraft. This we did all day, and realised that something was amiss in the world; perhaps doomsday in the making.

We fitted a weapon onto every aircraft on the unit, including, unusually, the OCU (Operational Conversion Unit) and BCDU (Bomber Command Development Unit) kites. As more people were brought in to cover the 'see-off' (should it ever occur, heaven forbid) the weapon load teams were mostly stood down. But first, we had the riot act read to us about not blabbing to the civilian populace about what we had been doing all day long.

Heck, if we were soon off to nuke the Russkies then I reckon that Joe Public would be finding out about it pretty soon. Oh well, if this was to be the ending of the world we thought that we would do the only thing left open to us. We went in to Doncaster to get drunk for the last time.

Whilst in the pub, the TV was on when there was a flash announcement on screen talking about some missile crisis in Cuba and that the Yanks and Russkies were having a real 'toe-to-toe' slanging match. Some statement had been made in the Houses of Parliament by some minister for propaganda or something, to the effect that whilst the British Government were monitoring the crisis, no action was being taken.

We all laughed at this and asked ourselves 'What the hell have we been doing all day, then?'

Since then, I have never believed a word of what politicians have said.

It was during this period that my mate, Dave Andrews, who was at Honington on Victors, had his once in a lifetime scare.

At 0200 hrs, he had to check out a 'nuke' that was loaded to a QRA (Quick Reaction Alert) aircraft. Inside the bomb bay was a long-range fuel tank as well as the bomb, which made things very tight; especially for Dave who has never been considered to be svelte. Further, as it was the middle of winter he had his full compliment of 'trog' boots, sea boot socks, thick woolly pully and 'Jacket Cold/Wet'.

He climbed into the bomb bay via the access door and managed to get past the tank to carry out his check of the bomb temperature readings (appropriately named 'yellow sun'). As he did his check his wet 'trog' boots slipped and he did a neat slide under the bomb with his legs trapped by his boots up the other side between the bomb bay doors and the bomb.

He was well and truly stuck.

The first thing that went through his mind was the film currently showing at the Astra, which was *Dr Strangelove*. In that film Slim Pickens did his rodeo-riding act on the back of the bomb as it fell to earth. If Kruschev had woken up in the night with indigestion, then Dave could well have been in the same situation as Slim Pickens.

He struggled for a good few hours before finally managing to extricate himself, having tried to attract the attention of the lone policeman a few aircraft along the row who, with his dog, were hiding in the lee of the undercarriage trying to get protection from the wind.

Years later he learned that the Yellow Sun bomb was particularly 'leaky' of its radiation and that him straddling the nuke (I suppose it was an inverse straddle as most people think of straddling something from above) for a number of hours meant that he should not, at least in theory, have been able to have children.

He is now pleased that he was able to do so.

Finningly started to hold 'Open Days' whilst I was there. The first one went well and I had been assigned to sell car-parking tickets. I handed in a lot more money than I had sold tickets as many of the drivers paid their money and then drove off not waiting for me to give them a ticket. I told this to the lads in the room.

The next year I was assigned to ticket selling again. A lad in my room, someone that I did not really like, said that he had been assigned to 'visiting aircraft' but did not want to do it. He asked me if I would swap duties with him as a favour. As I said, I didn't really like him so I said 'No'! He offered me £5 to swap duties as he really didn't want to do 'visiting aircraft'. I agreed and we swapped duties.

Scotty told me that I had been stupid to swap as the other guy only wanted to make money from the drivers who did not wait for their ticket. The penny tumbled and I realised that I had been conned. (I was still a naive young lad in many ways, not experienced in the ways of the world.) At the end of the day I asked him how much he had made for himself. He calmly replied that he had made £85, which was about three months wages for him as he was only an SAC.

This was the first time that I had come across such blatant dishonesty and it soured me towards some of the members of the RAF. However, it must be remembered that he was one of the last of the national servicemen and not a true RAF chappie.

I enjoyed the visiting aircraft bit though, and learned that not all Meteor jet aircraft had ejection seats and that the torpedo underneath the Swordfish was in fact a telegraph pole made up to look like the real thing.

I went into a tailors shop in Retford one day and asked if he could make me a jacket to my own design. Everyone at the time was wearing Italian style close fitting suits and I wanted to be different.

The tailor said that he could make me any style that I wanted and so I told him that I wanted a jacket with no lapels, the sleeve length and jacket length to be the same and a half belt built in at the back and the front shape of the edge a very exaggerated curve.

The tailor had it made and put it into the window awaiting me to pick it up.

When I eventually went to collect it, the tailor told me that he could have sold it many times over and would I mind if he made some more. I said that it didn't bother me and thought no more about it.

I wore my jacket and it caused a minor sensation wherever I went.

I remember that soon after, a group of us had gone to Edinburgh to Keith's wedding where I wore my trendy jacket. Keith's sister, who had only recently become engaged, took an instant fancy to me (must have been the jacket), so much so that as I slept on Keith's parents settee that night she came down in the middle of the night and gave me such a good time that I have always had a soft spot for Scottish lassies ever since.

About eight months later I saw The Beatles (the pop group, if any of you are too young to remember) wear 'my' jacket on the telly. Lo and behold, the next time that I walked past that tailors shop in Retford the front of the shop was emblazoned with 'TAILOR TO THE BEATLES'.

I threw the jacket in the bin in our room in disgust as I wasn't that interested in the Beatles, but it was fished out again by Mal who offered me £5 for it.

I had my first taste of royalty at Finningley. One day the Queen Mum (everything in the RAF is abbreviated so she was called 'TQM' i.e. The Queen Mother) decided that she would go to Donny races. It was a regular occurrence for a Royal Flight aircraft to lob in at Finningley when some big race was on. Anyway, I had been 'specially selected' (it was my turn!) to hold the umbrella for her if it rained while she de-planed.

Needless to say, it absolutely bucketed down. My instructions were that I was to hold the umbrella at arm's length whilst ensuring that the 'functional' part of it was over the royal head at all times. Eassssy.

Picture me at the top of the aircraft steps, already soaked to the skin, following TQM down the steps and across the apron. Without any warning whatsoever she shouts 'My plants!' and promptly zooms past me and back into the aircraft.

That girl can get a move on and she was no spring chicken then; it did not surprise me in the least that she lived to a grand old age, she was as fit as a fiddle. Needless to say, I try to catch her up but failed miserably.

Out of the aircraft she comes again, carrying a plantpot with some weed in it, gives me a little 'Am I not a silly girl!' sort of look and we start the whole kit and caboodle again, this time with success.

It was whilst driving into Donny after this incident, that a couple of guys leapt out in front of me as I drove past the racetrack. They were also soaked to the skin and said that their taxi had let them down and they had to get to the airport, which was only about three miles away. As they got in, one told me that his private aircraft was waiting (Yeah! I thought) and his pilot was Peter Twiss. (More Yeah! Yeah! I thought.)

As I dropped them off at the side of this small private jet (very rare in those days), out pops the very same Peter Twiss whom everyone of my generation would recognise due to his breaking of the World Speed Record in the FD2 (Fairy Delta). The guy that I had assumed to be 'all mouth and trousers' then stuffed a wad of notes, equivalent to about four months' wages, into my hand. I had never seen so many 'beer chits', and just for giving the guy a lift in my little 100E Ford Anglia.

One of the winters was really bad, and being the nation's nuclear deterrent, the runway had to be kept open at all costs. We had a piece of kit called the 'Sno-Flo' to help(?). This was a jet engine mounted sideways on a Type 'F' bomb trolley. The idea was that the hot efflux would melt the ice and blow it away. The trouble was that if the engine was blowing too hard then the whole trolley used to slide sideways. This meant that the engine could only be run on part power. Some of the other units had a far better idea. They had a jet engine mounted on either side and at the front of a fuel bowser, the advantage being that the weight of the bowser acted against the jet efflux. I suppose that it had some limitations, as all the ice was melted and thrown further down the runway, only to freeze again.

With our sideways Sno-Flo I suppose that most of the ice was blown off the runway instead of straight down it. Even so, a good deal of the ice was just melted, blown away and then refroze. This made it doubly difficult for us guys, as we believed that if we were just allowed to clear the snow and ice manually, chipping away with pick and shovel if necessary, and removing it before it was melted and refroze again as it was by the Sno-Flo, would have been far easier. Needless to say, management would not listen to us, thus their intransigence actually prevented us from achieving what they had set us out to do.

This line of management style seemed to prevail throughout the RAF then and still does so today. Management should say, 'achieve this' and leave it up to people more qualified than them to actually achieve it. A very simplistic view maybe, but what did officers know about shifting ice and snow; they had never done it!

The only advantage to the bad weather was the 'rum ration'. This was good old fashioned navy rum the consistency of treacle. We were each doled out an eighth of a pint which, when drunk, was like a red hot poker travelling down our throats, into the stomach, down into our toes and back up to the head. At that stage we were ready to shift snow and ice despite the efforts of management to make it as difficult as possible. We would show 'em!

Whilst at Finningley, my parents moved from Retford to Doncaster to set up a ladies' hairdressing business. It was something that my mother had wanted to do all of her life, and as dad had had an accident whilst sinking the mine shaft at Bevercoates Colliery, which prevented him working, they obviously thought that for my mum to run a business would be the ideal thing to do. They were very successful at this and life for them started to look good. As my mum employed a few girls and I used to go with them and my parents to the 'hairdressers balls', well, yes, things were pretty good for me as well.

At about this time, I started to work in the Ejection Seat bay, servicing 3KS (Vulcan) and 3A (Valiant) seats. At the time we used to both maintain the seats and carry out fitment and removals as well.

Fitting and removal of Vulcan seats was easy as we used to slide them up or down the rails after the riggers had removed the canopy. The rim of the cockpit was the only place that we could stand to guide the seat down the rail, the other guy being in the cockpit. It always seemed to be my job to stand on the rim, which is quite high, and there was never any safety harness. At least, I never thought that there was until I was almost knocked off the rim by the crane driver swinging the seat over the rim and far too close to me. I discovered that there was, in fact, an existing harness especially designed for us. I tried it the next time but the whole thing was so unwieldy and, I thought more dangerous, that I never used it again. Fitting and removal of the Valiant seats was also a pain. We had to struggle with them through the door of the aircraft and into the cockpit; there is not a lot of room in a Valiant cockpit!

Whilst servicing the seats in the bay, I learned that I had this uncanny knack of being able to unravel the lines on the 5-foot diameter drogue parachutes and pack them into the head boxes better, quicker and easier than anyone else. I was quite pleased at this because I don't think that I had excelled at anything before.

In the seat bay, I also learned a lesson about store-men, the supply system and me. We needed to carry out a modification to the seats and needed to demand some 'Tucker-pop' rivets. George, the Senior Technician 'boss' of the seat bay, told me to demand from stores enough rivets to do the mod. I sat down and worked out that we needed about 400 rivets. George told me to demand them against his inventory and to get a few spares over the 400. I decided that I would demand 500 rivets and put in the requisite piece of paper to the store-man.

All items in the RAF are issued with a 'D of Q' (Denomination of Quantity), which bore no resemblance (at least it didn't then) as to how the items were packaged. They were usually packaged in quantities of 1, 5, 10, 100 or gross or whatever. Even so the D of Q was usually 'each'. I didn't know the intricacies of this weird system of course, so I ordered 500.

A few days later the store-man came staggering in with a huge bag of rivets. We ended up with 500 **GROSS** of tucker-pop rivets.

As they were 'C' stores, i.e. expendables and issued against an inventory but not included in that inventory, the store-men would not take them back. Consequently, we ended up giving away bags full of very useful rivets to anyone who wanted them. The lesson that I learned from that was that store-men were stupid, the stores system was stupid, and I was stupid.

It was during this period, feeling quite pleased with myself for learning some lessons from the University of Life, that our group decided to go to the Danum Hotel in 'Dirty Donny' to the Saturday night dance.

It was there that I saw this vision in a white dress covered in large blue spots (the dress not the vision). She had blonde hair, albeit bottle blonde, in the 'bee-hive' style. As I looked at her it seemed as if some spotlight had been trained only on her, and everything and everybody else around was just a dull blur. She was the most beautiful girl I had ever seen. Even though I was not the dancing type of feller, I had to ask her for a dance so that I could get to know her. She was the girl destined to be my wife, the mother of my children.

I did not know at the time that this marriage would only last for 16 years, but who does. If people thought that their marriage was going to end there wouldn't be a lot of point in getting married in the first place.

We started going out together and she told me that she was a virgin. We quickly got engaged and she was a virgin no more. That was the way of things in those days; girls who were 'saving themselves' normally stopped saying 'No' once an engagement ring was on the finger.

The Air Force must have found out that I had just got engaged because they posted me.

The author, aged 19, at Finningley. All the girls used to ask me if I was Italian. I was supposed to look like Rory Calhoun.

4

RAF LYNEHAM, LECONFIELD, STAFFORD AND SCAMPTON

(The Working Week Review)

While at Finningley, and long before I met my 'bride-to-be', I had been asked if I would like to undertake 'Work Study' duties. Apparently, or so I was told, I had been specially selected as I was well qualified with my ONC. Off I went to do a month's course at Nottingham University, and came back as a Work Study Practitioner.

What a con! All that the RAF wanted was a tiny aspect of work study, in that they needed to know how many hours of productive work was undertaken by the Aircraft Tradesmen and how many hours of work was lost through sports, illness, leave, having haircuts, doing all the various duties that we had to do and things like that. So they decided to carry out a 'Working Week Review'.

This entailed teams of 'practitioners' sitting at tables and recording the amount of time that each man was at work, even if he was not actually working on aircraft or equipment he was still classed as being 'available for work' (just like being on the dole really, as that lot are all supposed to be 'available for work'). Each 'Practitioner' was responsible for about 7 or 8 men. We had groups of about 50 of us and we went to various units for 3 months at a time.

Our first station was Lyneham in Wiltshire, which had Comet and Britannia aircraft. I, along with two others, went to the Comet hangar and set up our table in the corner of the hangar. All of the Comet Maintenance Team members in the hangar were told that they were to come to us whenever they were going to go anywhere and explain to us what they were going to do. Similarly, they were to tell us when they got back. All that we had to do was write in a code on our sheet of paper into the appropriate 5 minute blocks against each individual. This was so ee-ee-sy.

To cap it all, I was promoted to the rank of Corporal Technician, which meant that I was in charge of our little group of 'practitioners'. A Corporal Technician had two stripes, just like an ordinary corporal, but yet again, the pointy bit pointed towards the head as we were 'Technicians', viz the clever types.

It soon became apparent that watching other people work while we in fact were sitting on our 'butts' watching them was excruciatingly boring. Still, someone had to do it, so I suffered having nothing to do for 'Queen and Country' and we just settled down to read books etc. I do not understand to this day why we needed three people to do this job, as one would have done just as well. Probably it was a throw-over from the civvies, who had taught us on the course; whilst we servicemen would have been OK doing the job with one person, in the civilian world, it needed three civvies to carry out the task or their Trade Union would have had them out on strike!

What the boredom of sitting down and doing nothing all day long meant, of course, was that we had to let off a bit of steam in the local hostelries during the evenings. I had my car; the same little Ford Anglia, so we used to go out in that.

I remember one night that we had been celebrating someone's impending demob. When it came to drive back to camp, I was driving up both left and right banks of the road that is the main high street of Wooton Basset. I decided that I really was not in a fit state to drive, and so I drove round to the local cop shop, not hitting anyone or anything on the way (or at least I don't think that I did).

We went inside and explained that we were from Lyneham, and I said something to the affect that I was too drunk to drive and would they lock us up in a cell for the night (there were four of us). I was amazed when they said that they would drive us back to Lyneham in a cop car, with another policeman driving my car. This they duly did.

Just like the yanks say, 'Aren't our policemen wonderful'. (Well at least they were then; I am not so sure about the ones now.)

As it was such a long way, I was driving back to Thorne, just outside Doncaster, where my fiancée (they were always called 'fancy' by us fellers) lived, about one weekend in four, staying at her parents' house. Which meant I was back at Lyneham for three weekends out of four plus the weekday nights; well, 'a man's gotta do what a man's gotta do ...' In my case it was to get my end away.

I remember one of the girls who seemed quite proud of the fact that she was frigid. I did my best on that girl; had her stripped starkers in the car, but could not, under any circumstances, get her 'going'.

It was quite a blow to my ego and confidence; so much so, that even though I did try to have my wicked way with her, it is just no fun whatsoever when she had not the slightest interest. I gave up on her and she was the first girl that I actually dumped; a trend that was to continue, as I was getting to the age where all the girls I met wanted to marry me (or whoever they were going out with at the time; all they really wanted was to be married to someone, almost anyone it seemed).

It was a very dangerous time for us fellers!

I remember one weekend, I went with John to his parents' place in Blackpool. They lived in the South Shore area. John took me to the local meeting place to pick up some crumpet; a place called the Queens Hotel in Cleveleys, I seem to recall. It turned out that the place was heaving with bodies, mostly, it seemed, of the female form.

This was heaven. Wall-to-wall totty! I asked John where all the boys were and he told me that the ones who were already 'fixed up', were with their girls somewhere else. Apparently the girls this night were the 'spares' of the town i.e. the additional number of the girls over the boys, due entirely to the influx of girls over the summer season who worked as waitresses, cleaners, cooks etc. that the hotel trade needed. We took a couple (one each; more than one at a time was to come later!) back with us to John's place.

His parents were the most broad-minded that I have ever met in my life, as it was his mother who suggested to the girls that they stay the night. These particular girls were on holiday in some chalet somewhere with another couple of girls, so it did not matter if they stayed out all night. John's mum said that the girls could have one room whilst John and I shared another. By the innuendo and look on her face, John's mother let it be known that she did not mind if we did not wake up in our respective locations.

I was bonking this girl (can't even remember her name) when the door opened and in walked John's mum and dad. They said something like 'you two are getting on well' and, after a couple of minutes looking at us, walked out again. 'Shocked and stunned' was not the word for it. (Yes, I know that shocked and stunned is two words but stop being pedantic and let me get on with my life!)

* * *

The Work Study Team had been at Lyneham for the allotted three months, so it was time to move on to the next unit that was due to be reviewed. This was to be Leconfield, just outside of Beverley in Yorkshire, the home of the Lightning and not far from the home of my fiancée.

One of the peculiarities of the Lightning aircraft, was that it was a 'spring' airframe. Take something from the aircraft and the airframe would spring into a different position and getting that component back again was hell. I had heard that sometimes it was necessary to 'open' the airframe with a crowbar to make things fit again.

There used to be some spectacular flying by Lightnings at the time, as all the visiting foreign dignitaries that the government were trying to sell the aircraft to were wheeled up to Leconfield. After watching the graceful landings of the Comet and Britannia at Lyneham, the 'controlled crash', as it was usually called (well, most were controlled, I think!), of the Lightning was a real eye opener. They were a mad lot those Lightning pilots; no wonder that the aircraft was nicknamed 'Frightening' by the lads who worked on them.

The period at Leconfield was during the height of the summer and I recall that it was a hot one. There seemed to be lots of leafy villages in the area with some great village pubs. Quite a soporific time was Leconfield. Not a lot of extra nookie, as I was seeing my fiancée every weekend, but a very mellow time.

Three months at Leconfield and we were then off to Stafford (yes, in Staffordshire). This was the home of 16 MU (Maintenance Unit), which consisted of five separate sites spread over quite a large area.

My little team of three went to 2 Site, which consisted of about 15 store-men and lots of huge storage buildings. There was no repair work carried out on this site so the manpower involved was quite small; all that they had to contend with was storage, which also involved issues and receipts of, usually, a lorry-load at a time. The store-men were in and out of buildings all day long either putting something in or taking something out or just sweeping it to keep it clean. It was an impossible task trying to keep tabs on them so we had to rely on them completely to tell us what they were doing.

The three of us spent most of our days sitting around drinking tea and talking or reading the good old book. We used to wander around the buildings every now and then to relieve the boredom and to stretch our legs and have a chat to the store-men for a change; well, we would if we could find one, that is. All of the buildings used to be unlocked and open during the day, no doubt to ventilate them, and closed and locked again every night.

Stafford town itself was quite boring. I was not scoring too well with the local talent, apart from the odd WRAF or two (no, I am not saying that WRAF's were odd!) and to be honest, I hardly ever seemed to fancy the Stafford girls. In any case, I was still driving to Thorne most weekends to be with my fiancée so I suppose that my 'urges' were being satisfied anyway and I was getting quite used to having sex on tap.

It was about this time that the RAF decided to change the rank structure. Up until now had been a twin route system of technical and command ranks as shown below:

In theory, an SAC could be promoted direct to Corporal, but this

Technician stream		Command stream
Master Technician		Warrant Officer
Chief Technician		Flight Sergeant
Senior Technician		Sergeant
Corporal Technician		Corporal
Junior Technician		
	Senior Aircraftsman	
	Leading Aircraftsman	

rarely happened in the technical trades. However, once a Junior Technician you could take technical exams and get promoted up the technical ladder on a time basis, or wait for promotion on the command ladder. The time basis was 3 years from Junior Technician to Corporal Technician, 4 years from Corporal Technician to Senior Technician, 5 years from Senior Technician to Chief Technician and 6 years or more from Chief Technician to Master Technician.

Most opted for the technical ladder as the technical folk were paid more than the command folk. This was true all the way up the ladder. A Chief Technician was the same rank level as a Flight Sergeant but the Chief was paid more.

The theory being that the 'techie' could tell the command type how to do something and the command type could tell the 'techie' when to do it.

However, after the powers that be decided to do away with the 'techie' side except for Junior Technician and Chief Technician, which was maintained, the new rank structure for the technical trades therefore looked like this:

Warrant Officer
Flight Sergeant
Chief Technician
Sergeant
Corporal
Junior Technician
Senior Aircraftsman
Leading Aircraftsman

Now some of the old wartime Flight Sergeants, for example, had turned their stripes upside down and got paid more for being a 'techie'. These people now found themselves below their original rank and now also getting paid less money. The argument was always that the needs of the RAF must come first. It is always this argument when it only affects airmen. If it had affected the officers the problem would have received more support.

I took my uniform home to mum to ask her to turn my stripes over to be an ordinary Corporal instead of being a Corporal Technician. She was upset as she was convinced that I had been demoted; especially after all the things that I had said about the stripes pointing towards my head.

* * *

I was still driving my little Anglia, but one of 'my lads' used to drive a brand new Ford Zodiac.

He was an LAC (Leading Air Craftsman, which despite its fancy sound was actually the lowest rank in the air-force) and it used to cause a few problems for us. Riding around in his car in uniform involved lots of improper salutes, as people thought that we were VIPs, after all, the AOC's (Air Officer Commanding, usually an Air Vice Marshal) staff car was the same shape but a lowlier version, and not many officers could afford a car like that.

How an LAC came to have such a grand car was simple; he used to work in night-clubs as an entertainer at nights. His RAF job was only a day job and, as LACs did not do any sort of RAF duties then that involved having to work at night, it meant that every night he was off blowing his trumpet, cracking jokes and getting paid a Group Captain's wages for doing it. Needless to say, he couldn't wait until demob.

At the end of my stint at Stafford I had decided that I was now old enough to be married. In any case, all my mates were getting married and I was getting left behind. I was already engaged so my fiancée seemed to be the obvious choice of girl to marry. You have to realise that fellers like me got engaged not because they wanted to marry the girl in question, but because, like I said earlier, 'ring around finger means knickers around ankle'.

By this time I had moved to Scampton in Lincolnshire, which was only a stone's throw from Thorne. We got married around the time that Winston Churchill died. Our honeymoon was to London and as we were walking around, we came upon this huge queue. It turned out to be the queue to see 'Winnie' lying in state. I said to my wife 'let's join the queue to see him,' and she went storming off in a huff. It was at this point I realised that she was devoid of a sense of humour.

Scampton was another home for the Vulcan, just like Finningley. Still, as before, all we had to do was watch other people work.

I had heard about how the RAF 'people-posting people' (i.e. the shinies at the RAF Records Office) did not like airmen to get married as it cost them money. We were convinced that they thought that any extra money paid to us would be taken out of their own pockets. We used to get married man's allowance in those days which boosted our pay by about 40%. The rumours around the RAF at the time were that as soon as someone got married and the RAF had to pay them extra money, then the individual ended up on a one-year unaccompanied overseas posting, the marriage broke down and by the time that the individual returned to UK he was single again. This happened time after time to people that I knew, so I suppose that it should not have been any surprise to me that within three months of marriage I was in Bahrain on a one-year unaccompanied posting.

Quite apart from having to leave my new bride, I also had to sell my little Ford Anglia.

5

RAF MUHARRAQ

(The Mighty Hunter)

Muharraq was a small island next to the main island of Bahrain in the Persian Gulf and joined to it by a causeway. When we landed in our 'Whispering Giant' (Britannia), before the aircraft doors were opened, the aircraft cabin was given a good spray of DDT, to supposedly kill any bugs that had hitched a ride from the UK with us. But now we know that DDT kills humans as well as the bugs so the Air Force has probably reduced my chances of survival to a 'ripe old age' to absolute nil. When the doors were finally opened, as well as choking on the DDT fumes, the heat and humidity hit us like a brick, it was so very oppressive.

All the new arrivals, or 'moonies', so called due to the moon colour of their faces and the rest of their bodies (i.e. white), spent the first few days in transit accommodation. In reality, this was an old mud-walled, wooden-floored, grass-roofed mini zoo. The whole place was alive with insects and other creepy crawlies, which revelled in fresh English blood.

Luckily, 'transit' was only a temporary measure and I soon moved into a Twynam, which was part of the Squadron accommodation complex and was to be my home for the next year. The Twynam was a hut with a shiny aluminium skin externally on the walls and roof to reflect away the sun's rays and therefore the heat. The roof extended about 6 feet further out than the walls; this was to provide shade for the windows and walls to keep the heat of the sun out. The floor was concrete to prevent the bugs from climbing through the cracks in wooden floors, like they did in transit, and the walls were of a chipboard type construction (unpainted) that the bugs did not like to eat.

Most important was the fact that the rooms were air conditioned. Bliss!

Nevertheless, we still had to stand the legs of our beds in four tins of paraffin to prevent the bugs from climbing up into bed to join and devour us.

There were about 8 beds per room. The first impression on entering was one of total darkness. Outside was glaring bright sunlight and it took a few seconds for our eyes to adjust to the gloom. Even so, the rooms always had a gloominess about them, even when the door was opened. However, as the room was air-conditioned the unwritten rule was that the door was to be opened for the minimum amount of time. Some 'chowgi wallah' (Indian) was always opening the door with his pathetic wail of 'Coffee John' as he tried to sell us a cup of his revolting coffee that he carried in an urn on his back. He always got the same abuse from our room and it transpires from almost every room on camp. Poor feller was only trying to make a living.

Work was to be on 208 Squadron, which was equipped with the Hunter FGR9. We had a small hangar in which to carry out scheduled maintenance and rectification on the planes, which, unless they were on Primary or Minor servicing in the hangar, used to spend their daylight hours either on the pan in a nice neat row or in the air.

The 'Line Hut' was an old engine box, so the Line and OOP's (Out Of Phase) Controller used to spend their working days with their bondu (desert) boots full of their own sweat. The crew room was a Twynam type building which had a 'Tea-bar' with a 'fridge that sold 'Stims'. 'Stims' were a local lemonade/orangeade type drink, but we could also buy other cold drinks like Tango, which was a lot more expensive than the local 'stims' (we had Tango in Bahrain years before it was introduced into the UK) and the ubiquitous coke.

On the last Friday of every month we had a 'beer call'. The boss used to fly to Masirah and would bring back a load of crayfish in the Sabrinas. (Sabrinas were the 'protuberances' on the 'chest' of the Hunter that the gun ammunition links used to be collected in during firing.) Crayfish were the size of small lobsters and were very tasty, especially with beer in the other hand. It was during one of these 'beer calls' that I recall a young jockey (pilot) telling me a lesson that he had learned about not taking things at face value.

He was flying escort to one of the Beverley transport aircraft down route and he was chatting to the Bev pilot over the radio. Talk took to discussing the relative merits of each aircraft and the Hunter pilot started rabbit-ing on about how the Hunter was more interesting to fly due to its manoeuvrability, acceleration and speed.

The Bev pilot said that he could do a few tricks in his old kite that the fighter pilots could never match. When asked to demonstrate the Bev pilot said 'You just watch.'

After a few minutes the Bev pilot comes back on the air and said 'Did you see that?'

Not having seen a thing the Hunter pilot asks what was so wonderful that he had done.

The Bev pilot answers 'Well I went for a little stroll, got a coffee and went downstairs for a chat with the Load-master.'

The Hunter pilot never boasted about his aircraft again. Anyway, the Bev could do something that normal aeroplanes could never do; it used to reverse itself into its parking slot on the line as it had reverse pitch on its propellers.

It took a while of being in Bahrein for us to actually drink hot tea or coffee again. We were usually at the 'hairy knees' stage by then. It's not until you go overseas and live in shorts permanently that you realise that hair actually grows on the knees but that long trousers constantly rubbing on the knee wear them off. Subsequently, the title of 'moony' given to all newcomers was not used for people who had hairy knees. Some people never did get a tan due to sweating so much but everyone got hairy knees. It is only after you had been in Bahrain for a while and watched the latest batch of newcomers step off the plane that you realised how sickly a white skin looks. No wonder we Brits spend so much money trying to get a tan.

I enjoyed the work on the squadron; squadron camaraderie was excellent and I had two of my very own Junior Technicians to work for me. Our little empire was mostly 'wrecks and sheds'. (Rectification and Scheduled Maintenance), although we did keep getting pulled onto the line to help out with 'liney' work.

The other squadron on the island was 30 Squadron flying the afore-mentioned Beverley as I have said. I use the term 'flying' loosely, because they were renowned for always being constantly sick. Beverleys seemed to do most of their flying ferrying new engines and 'sooties' (Propulsion tradesmen) down route somewhere in the Middle East to fix another Bev which had gone dead somewhere.

There were also a couple of PR (Photo Recce) Canberras on permanent detachment from 13 Squadron in Cyprus, but they spent most of their time wrapped up in mothballs, flying only on rare occasions. Also on the camp were a load of 'Paras', presumably to jump out of the Bevs, but I never saw them do that and the least said about the 'grunts' the better. All they ever seemed to want to do was to cause 'aggro'; friend or foe alike.

* * *

Work on the squadron was the usual thing that armourers do; load the guns, which in the case of the Hunter was to replace the whole gun pack, load 3-inch concrete (usually) head rockets and fit and remove 100-gallon or 230-gallon drop tanks. There was the usual scheduled servicing of course, that I was responsible for, which involved replacement of aircraft weapon components like ERUs (Ejector Release Units), EMRUs (Electromagnetic Release Units), Ejection Seats and various other bits and pieces.

However, most of the work seemed to be removal of the ejection seats so that some other trade guy could get to his bit of kit to fix or replace it. This usually happened at the end of the flying day as the air-crew used to carry 'snags' (faults) through to then and only when they went off for the day did they start to raise job cards to rectify the faults, that sometimes took all night to fix, when the aircraft should have been grounded when it first occurred. This is a typical attitude of the air-crew; so long as they got their games in the air they never gave a damn for the ground-crew working all hours to fix their toys.

(What is the difference between God and Pilots? God doesn't think he's a pilot!)

What this meant of course, was that we could only refit the seat again when the other guy had finished. Therefore, we were always the last to finish work, 'cos when the other guy had done his bit and went off back to his hut and bed then we had to re-fit the seat, do Vital Checks, get a sneck (SNCO) to do his Independent Check and only then, after we had 'signed up' the job cards of course, could we knock off for the day.

One day I went for my lunch in the mess. I was particularly hungry that day. In fact we were always hungry as the food was really bad: Bromide in the tea, powdered milk, injected eggs, pom (powdered mash potato long before and nowhere near as good as the present day stuff like 'Smash'), hard tack biscuits that were the home for weevils etc.

We only used to eat the biscuits after banging the edge of it on the table a few times so that the weevils came out of the biscuit to see what the hell was going on. Give them a few seconds to get to the outside of the biscuit, tap the biscuit on the edge of the table again and all the weevils fell off. Only then was it relatively safe to eat hard tack biscuit. Some of the new comers used to eat the biscuits before 'de-weeviling' but they eventually learned the score after watching the 'old timers'. Most of the food used to have little bugs in of some sort, the philosophy being that if you could see little bugs on the food you could get most of them off and that the little bugs had already eaten the tiny bugs that could not be seen which would probably do more harm to the body anyway.

The best meal of the day was supper, which we used to make ourselves. We would toast bread, cover it in jam and make cocoa and fill ourselves as much as possible with that. The soup in the mess was reasonable except when the air conditioning broke down, which seemed to be most of the time. When this happened we had to eat our soup as quickly as possible as it was so hot and humid that as we leaned forward to drink our soup the sweat used to run down our foreheads, onto our noses, drip off our noses and into the soup.

Consequently, if soup was not eaten quickly then we never actually finished it as the bowl was filled up with sweat as quickly as we drank the contents.

I digress, I started to talk about this particular trip to the mess. Right, I went for my plate of food, which was chicken, peas and pom. Like I said, I was really hungry that day so I put this very first big forkful of pom in my mouth and started to chew, when it crunched.

Now I may not be the brightest of folk but I do know that mashed potato is not supposed to crunch. Removal of the lump revealed a big black beetle. They were commonly known as 'shit beetles' due to the fact that was where they usually made their home. Needless to say I did not eat any more of that meal, in fact I didn't eat anything until supper, which I made myself so that I could ensure that the food was de-bugged.

I struck up a friendship with a guy called 'Chitty', so called because he was always on the lookout for chitty boxes. Now chitty boxes were the boxes that we used to get our belongings shipped out to us from the UK in, and at the end of our tour we could then send a chitty box back to UK with our 'goodies' in. The box that we brought out usually rotted by the time it was required again so when people came out from the UK they would pass on their box to someone who was about to go home. 'Chitty' made the management of chitty boxes an obsession and used to 'negotiate' deals with incoming and outgoing personnel.

Anyway, Chitty and I would go to the pool at about 0530 hrs each morning for a swim. He was really into swimming and his speciality stroke was the butterfly. He had shoulders about six feet across and was one of the early exponents of the 'porpoise' style of stroke. It was Chitty who taught me to swim as I had not been allowed anywhere near water as a child due to my glandular fever. I learned to swim quite well and we used to have the pool to ourselves at that time of day.

A new Station Master (it was the Station Commander really and they were Group Captains) was posted in and he had 3 daughters of 14, 16 and 18. Now there were very few women on the island, apart from the locals who hated us and anyway, all that you could see of them were two eyes, the rest being covered in black.

The 'Groupie's daughters decided that they too would go swimming at 0530 hrs in the morning, and the sight of 3 pretty white-skinned girls clad in bikinis really set us up for the day. Needless to say, we used to do a bit of ogling, which the girls seemed to enjoy. (We certainly did!)

Things got a little out of hand though when the girls started swimming up to us and 'touching' us on the only bit of material that we were wearing. Obviously, we were initially thrilled at this, but one of the sisters said that she was going to tell her dad that we had been touching them.

This was a risk that we, as mere Junior NCOs, were not going to take. We also came to the conclusion that what the girls really wanted was the pool to themselves. (The older ones were already getting screwed by the officer corps.)

We did the only thing that we could do and decided not to go to the pool again at that time of day. However, we did tell all the rest of the guys on camp the time that the girls went to the pool and, funny old thing, 0530 hrs became the most popular time for swimming. About a month later the Groupie banned everyone from the pool, except his daughters of course, until 0700 hrs, which is when we all started work anyway.

Chitty and I used to partner each other at bridge. Everybody at Muharraq used to play bridge to pass the time. There was not really a lot to do and boredom was everywhere.

We bought an old Vauxhall Velox that was more rust than metal and spent a lot of time trying to keep that thing going. Petrol in Bahrain was only 6d (2½p) a gallon so we used to bomb around the place a bit on the rare occasion that it was mobile. We then 'acquired' an old Austin 7 two-seater Chummy, but we never had much joy with that as it never used to work properly, so one day we drove it into the sea and just left it; shame really as they are worth a lot of money now.

One day the wind was howling and the sea very rough. Muharraq was a flat plate of land that was about 3 feet above sea level at its highest point and we could walk out to sea for about a mile and still be only up to our knees in water, but further out from that the land just dropped down to the middle of the world (or so it seemed). When the wind blew the sea used to be whipped up and hit the shelf about a mile out. Huge waves came crashing onto camp and used to flood the place. One weekend whilst this was happening, Chitty and I decided to paddle out in a two-seat canoe. We fought our way out against the crashing waves and it was great fun. I had never been in a canoe before and it was only after we got to the spot where the sea hit the shelf that Chitty decided that there was no way that we could get through the mountain of water to the relative calm on the other side.

By a series of shouts it was decided that we would have to turn around and that it was imperative that we complete the turn between waves. This did not seem possible to me as the waves only seemed to be about the length of the canoe apart. But, as death by drowning was the only other option (not really, as I have already said that the water was only about knee high), it spurred us on to make the most rapid turn in the history of canoeing, and here I am to tell the tale. Boy did my arms ache after that turn.

It has been said many times that 'mad dogs and Englishmen go out in the mid-day sun'. Well, in that case, we had to keep up the image. Our normal working hours were from 0700 hrs until 1300 hrs. We had breakfast before we went to work and had lunch after we left work. At about 1100 hrs we would have a 'Stim' and a roll that one of the lads who was running the Tea Bar would make. Sometimes we worked in the afternoon as well if the air-crew had really badly broken their trusty steeds, but in the main, the afternoons were free and we could do whatever we wanted.

The pool was standing room only at that time of day so some people would have an afternoon nap like all the Arabs did (it seemed to us that the Arabs had afternoon naps morning, noon and night), but quite a few 'mad Brits' went out for a walk. Now the afternoon walk became almost a ritual for some people. We (yes, it was a ritual for me also) all dressed the same in shorts, flip-flops and sweat towel which was worn either round the neck or tucked into the waist band of our shorts. There were two types of walks; 'Oggin troggin' and 'Bondu bashin'.

Oggin was the name we gave to the sea so oggin troggin was basically paddling around the beach area. Whilst this may sound exotic, we were officially banned from going into the sea as it was so disgusting. The Arabs did not have any form of sewerage system or waste disposal so everything went into the sea. Muharraq village was next to the camp and they dumped everything right on their own, and our, doorstep. One day, Chitty and I were 'troggin' when we came across a dead baby Arab girl floating in the water. It surprised neither of us and, after checking to ensure the poor mite really was dead, we just carried on walking. Needless to say, the first thing that we always did after 'oggin troggin' was to have a good shower.

The other type of walk was quite literally over the desert. The desert was called 'The bondu' so 'bondu bashin' was just walking over the desert. This was sometimes a bit of a problem as the local kids, if they were not having their afternoon kip, used to stone us. Luckily, the stones in that area of bondu were only small and we could run faster than they could, so all that was hurt was our pride.

We had an open-air cinema on camp and films were changed about twice per week. Being open air meant that in the cooler part of the year we used to take a blanket to wrap up in as well as the usual pillow to sit on. Sitting with a blanket around the shoulders with our feet on the seat, sort of 'hunched-up', provided great privacy to the individual.

Most of the guys were married but of course their wives were 6,000 miles away. Now, never to have had something in the first place means that it is not missed when it is no longer there, but to have nookie with your wife on a regular basis and then to have that taken away, makes things pretty hard. Perhaps that phrase is not very appropriate for what I am saying, but the proverbial 'hard-on' used to occur at all sorts of times of day and night. Even though the mess laced the tea with bromide. Watching a film with females in it, almost any female would suffice, was a big turn on. *It doesn't take much imagination to guess what went on under the privacy of the blanket.*

Behind the concrete block that acted as the screen, was one of the Sheik's houses, which used to house one of his minor harems. The house had a flat roof and the edge of the little wall surrounding the roof used to fill up with round little black blobs of cloth, each with a binocular in front of it. They used to watch the guys 'at play'. I wonder if they were doing something similar?

What a shame that they were frustrated because of a sheik who was getting old and probably took about a year to get around to screwing everyone in his harem, and yet only 20 yards away was an inexhaustible supply of randy and frustrated fellas.

* * *

We used to go off to Manama, the capital 'city' of Bahrain, to break the monotony and to do a bit of local shopping, not that there was all that much to buy. Most of the shops in the Suques sold 'gift' type things and a few stalls used to sell onions. Heaven knows what the locals used to eat apart from onions and fish. One day we were wandering through the Suque when I saw a shop selling sweet jars, you know, the big ones that they have in old fashioned sweet shops, full to the top with gold coins. Every type of gold coin you could imagine from Sovereigns, those Marie Theresa things, US Dollars and any other type of gold coin. When you think that once upon a time, all of our oil was bought using gold coins, as the Arabs would not, at the time, accept paper money, you can imagine that the Gulf States were awash with gold coins. Anyway, in I go to enquire about the cost of a $20 gold coin. The little Arab tells me the price and I work out that by the time I changed from Rupees (the local currency at the time) to Sterling and then the exchange rate between the US Dollar and Sterling, a $20 dollar gold coin would be costing me slightly less than $20. I bought one, only one, mind you, and I recently sold that $20 gold coin at auction and received the princely sum of £300. How I wish now that I had bought the whole sweet jar, or at least a jam jar, full of the things.

The squadron used to go on detachment very regularly. At least once per month we would be off to somewhere. Mostly to Sharja in the Trucial Oman States. Sharja camp had very few permanent people and was just a staging post. The squadron went as much to show a presence as anything but I do recall that we did most of our gunnery there.

The main thing that I recall about Sharja was the bread. It used to be made locally by a little Arab who actually seemed to like us. No doubt he made a lot of money from us as we would each eat a whole loaf of bread every day of the detachment, covered with jam if available but on its own if not. We didn't use butter or margarine as it just ran through the bread and out of the other side.

Sharja was also the home of Sheik Robbie. He was not a real sheik but he was a real rob dog. He was the local silversmith and used to make and sell anything that we wanted. Everybody used to buy filigree silver bits from him to take home to wives/girlfriends and parents.

That was of course if any of the guys remained married or had their girlfriend after a year of separation. Most of the girls used to end up sending a 'Dear John'. This was a letter that said that the relationship was over, usually because the girl could not wait for a year and had found someone else. All the 'Dear John' letters would be pinned up on the board along with a photo and an earlier letter where she would pledge her undying love forever. The unfortunate recipient usually also added a note about how the girl was only a slut anyway so 'what the heck'.

When the board became full, the oldest would be taken down and pasted in the 'Dear John' book that remained available for all to see.

All mail would be delivered to the workplace. Needless to say, whenever mail arrived, all work ceased and people sat down somewhere quiet and completely alone to open their letters hoping that it was not a 'Dear John'.

Life, and the female of the species, can be very cruel!

During our detachments to Sharja we would get at least one afternoon off when we would all go to a place called Khan Creek. This was a narrow inlet where the sea, when there was an incoming tide, used to race through to fill a large lake. It was great fun to swim out to sea and lie on our backs and let the tide take us inland. We would then walk back and repeat the whole process. All very simple stuff but like I said before, people were very bored and this was the extent of our excitement.

We were not crazy enough to do the reverse when the tide went out, so at that point we would all fool around kicking balls or whatever on the beach. One day, when we had stopped our flotation due to the turn of the tide, someone shouted 'Look, sharks'. Sure enough, there were a whole load of fins about 20 yards out from the shore.

Some idiot shouted 'Let's go and get them!' and every man jack of us leapt into the sea and started to swim after the sharks.

Luckily for us the sharks turned around and went away because when we came back ashore we realised that none of us had even got a penknife between us, and the sharks could have had a field day. It's amazing what people do to break the monotony.

We went on detachment to Salalah, which is round the Gulf a little bit more on the way to Aden, one time during the Radfan crisis. The aircraft usually had 100-gallon drop tanks fitted, but at Salalah they needed the extra range provided by the big 230-gallon tanks. They were loaded with High Explosive Ammo and HE rockets instead of 'ball' and concrete head rockets that were used during training. The aircraft would struggle into the sky with all the extra weight and when they got back an hour later the engines were sucking fumes and all the rocket racks and guns were empty.

One day whilst out there, my lads and I were fitting 230-gallon drop tanks. Now fitting drop tanks, of either type, was a fiddly enough process that involved removing the pin that secures the ERU jaw, lifting up the tank and refitting the jaw and pin. This meant that the NCO (me), would do the tricky bit and the two lads would lift the nose and tail of the tank. It was common that some days it was impossible to get the pin in, so we would do a swap of positions and somebody else would try. Sometimes it would be so bad that everybody would fail to fit the pin, the NCO or the next man would try again and the pin would eventually go straight in.

This particular day was like that and I had been fiddling for a couple of minutes trying to get the pin in without success. I said to Andy who was holding the nose of the tank 'Here, you have a go'. The two lads put the tank on the floor and we swapped positions.

As soon as Andy got into the same position that I had occupied a few seconds before, there was a 'crack' and Andy dropped down dead. Shot! An Arab had sighted on me but shot Andy when we changed positions. We picked up our rifles and blasted off a magazine at god knows what but I don't think that we were successful and by this time the RAF Regiment (Rock Apes) were screaming off in hot pursuit in their Land-Rover.

Life takes on a different view after something like that. There but for a couple of seconds go I!

One evening I thought that I had got some sand in my eye. I went to the mirror and rubbed around a bit and saw what I thought were little yellow maggots.

'No', says I and have another little wriggle of the eyelid. Sure enough, there they were again, little yellow maggots that wriggled their way back under my eyelid. Off I go to Sick Quarters and arouse the Duty Medic. He does not see anything and said for me to report sick in the morning. This I duly did and the MO (Medical Officer), a Para Captain who had been given the gen (information) about my complaint, looked in my eye whilst I rubbed the eyelid where the little beasts were hiding. He looked, blinked, and then, to my utter amazement, started hopping around the room on one leg and clapping his hands in glee shouting 'Yes, you've got it, you've got Loa-Loa.'

Oh good, thinks I, at least someone was pleased.

The MO calmed down a bit and called in everyone in Sick Quarters to come and have a look. This they all duly did and all got very excited (strange lot). The MO told me to go back to work but be ready for other people to see me.

For the next 4 weeks I kept getting phone calls to report to Sick Quarters so that everyone and his dog on the island could see my maggots. The MO finally said that the Institute of Tropical Medicine in London would need to see me. Great, thinks I, a trip back to dear old blighty.

Eventually however, two senior quacks from the Institute of Tropical Medicine flew out to Bahrain to see me, gave me a little box of pills and within two days my little friends had disappeared.

Apparently only one person in the world gets Loa-Loa each year and for 1965 I was he. Seemingly I was also the first white man to ever get it, so I must be in the Guinness Book of Records – World Health Organisation version.

Some claim to fame!

During the latter part of our tour we had to apply for an 'Area of Choice' for our posting back to the UK. It is a joke and everyone knows it, but we had to fill in the forms anyway. As we were on a one year unaccompanied, so-called 'hardship' tour we were supposed to get a preference to give us our choice.

I applied for the 'Doncaster area' as first choice, 'Yorkshire' for second and 'England' for third choice. We were also asked to give a negative choice and I put down 'Not outside England'. Now let's face it, that should have given them a huge choice to play with. Yet again, it came as no surprise when I got my posting. Ballykelly in Northern Ireland here I come.

6

RAF BALLYKELLY
(Shackletons don't bother me)

'Wifey' had thrown a big party for me upon my return from the desert. We had the bash in Moorends Working Men's Club, which was a miners' club. All servicemen are affiliated to the CIU working mens' clubs and in any case, her dad, an ex-miner just like mine, had been a lifelong member.

We had spent a couple of weeks at her parents' place and carrying out all of the 'duty visits', when it was time for us to set off to Ireland. We had already been allocated a married quarter at Ballykelly, as the unit had just had a load of new ones built. Ours was Number 14, Fort Drive and we were the first tenants. It was a 'B' type quarter, which meant that it had two bedrooms.

I drove from Thorne to Ballykelly (it was always called 'BK'), via the Stranraer-Larne ferry. This was quite a long journey as I had bought a second hand Morris JU 250 minibus that I had started to convert into a camper van. The camper van did not turn out to be a particularly successful venture, as 'wifey' was not very adventurous and we never did go camping in it. She had this paranoid fear of worms, which made her scream just at the sight of one. She was convinced that worms were going to crawl into the camper van just to frighten her.

She was pleased with the quarter, as everything was new and fresh. But before long, the newness and novelty soon began to wear off and she started to get homesick. She got worse and started talking about going home with or without me, and if it was without me then she wanted a divorce.

I put this problem down to the fact that she had only ever lived in a small mining village and just about the furthest that she had ever been was to Doncaster, all of 20 miles away, where she met me. To travel to foreign parts like Ireland was completely alien to her. We ended up travelling all the way back to Thorne, but after only a few days at her parents' place, she said that she wanted to go 'home', home of course being Ballykelly. Just like a women I suppose; fickle (I am sometimes pleased to say).

She did settle down a bit after our return but was not happy and our relationship was not at its best. Additionally, she was disgruntled that she was not allowed to work, so she got bored. To work in Northern Ireland you had to have a work permit and these were not given to the English. We were classed as foreigners. We were not allowed to go over there to work but the Irish, from both North and South, could come to England and could work anywhere they wanted to. Where is the justice in that?

I started work in the gun bay. These were the 20mm Hispano guns that were fitted in the nose turret of the Shackleton. Two guns per turret.

The Shack was an anti-submarine aircraft and the guns were the only armament that the aircraft could use if the submarine actually came to the surface. The rest of the armament was all designed for use when the sub was below the surface, and rumour had it that an enemy submarine would surface if it knew it was being attacked by a Shack as the submarines guns were more capable of shooting down the Shack than the other way round.

The poor old Shack was getting old even in BK days. All that flying at zero feet above the sea for hours on end used to get everything covered in salt water spray; it played havoc with alloy and dural components, which of course was about 99% of the aeroplane. The poor old riggers used to spend all of their days trying to keep corrosion to a minimum, as well as try to keep up with their favourite pastime of rotating rivets. The Shack was well known as '30,000 rivets flying in loose formation'. All the riggers carried about their person a scriber and spent any spare few minutes rotating rivets. I seem to recall that unless the rivet rotated a full 360 degrees it was not classed as loose. Moreover, there had to be a certain number within a certain run that had to be loose before any rectification work was carried out. I think that it had to be something like 5 in a run of 10 or with at least 4 adjacent to each other, or something like that.

Anyway, I digress. It wasn't long before I graduated into the Carrier Bay and the Sonobuoy Carrier became my speciality. Fred Savage, the chief iccy (IC, viz In Charge) of the bay actually told me off once for servicing the carriers too well. They went from me to the squadrons in as near perfect condition, including being re-painted, as possible; I was spending too much time trying to be a perfectionist. It was soon after this that the Squadron Leader called me into his office (I think that Fred wanted rid of this trouble maker 'cos I told him that I would not lower my standards for him or anyone else.) and said that he wanted to send me on a Torpedo course. This was a great honour as Torps were the most interesting of all jobs.

By the time that I went on my Torp course, I was the owner of a Triumph Spitfire car. 'Wifey' wanted something more 'suitable'. (She still would not go camping in our beat-up old camper.) Off I drove for a month's electronic lead-in course at the 'College of Knowledge' at RAF Newton in Nottinghamshire.

Here I learned the black art of Split Beam Oscilloscopes and Power Factor Correction and all about 'electric string'. Additionally, we learned how to recognise a resistor value using the 'Black Boys Rape Our Young Girls But Virgins Go Without' aide memoire. (I always thought that it was called a 'Rebus' but apparently it is not.)

What was more important was that the city of Nottingham was just a few miles down the road. Nottingham always had a reputation for having a young female population that was far bigger than the young male population, due apparently to the lace-making industry. As I was a young male I obviously had to help out the poor girls and me being a sporty Spitfire driver gave me a bit of an edge over the other guys. Now nookie in a Spitfire is not impossible but it is damn difficult. Luckily, the course was during decent weather so the girl and I would drive out to the country and screw in Sherwood Forest. I had three of them whilst on that course and very nice they were too.

Immediately after the lead-in course we were straight off to RAF St Mawgan in Cornwall to learn about the Mk30 and Mk44 Torpedo. I knew about Newquay from my Halton days and here I was, just a few miles outside Newquay for two months during the summer period. Bliss!

Yet again the Spitfire was a magnet for the girls and me being a perfect gentleman, well, when they wanted me to show them around for the week I could only oblige; and yes, they obliged me in that special way that only a girl can. It is often said that variety is the spice of life! I enjoyed my Torpedo Course!

* * *

After graduation from the course it was back to Ballykelly (and wife) and work in the Torpy Bay. Everyone in the bay was a Sneck (Senior Non Commissioned Officer, viz SNCO, viz Sneck) except me and I was still a Corporal. I started working on the old Mk30 with a guy called 'Butch' Pring. We had a set quantity of torps to service during each month and for the first two weeks or so we used to work like stink to get our quota finished. This was completely alien to the Irish philosophy, which is: 'Don't do today what you can put off until tomorrow'.

Having all of our work completed meant of course that for the remainder of the month we had no 'official' work to do. There was always something cropping up of course but in the main we had a lot of spare time to do the important things in life; like service the car, build radios and generally make all sorts of things for ourselves. These jobs were known as 'gash' jobs. I made my workbench during this time and it is still in use, thirty five years later, as good as new.

We always left the last torp of the month to be serviced in a stripped down state all over the workshop. This meant that whenever the boss walked in we could look as if we were hard at work on a torp.

Because torps were security classified the workshop doors were always kept locked. Whenever the Sqdn Ldr was going to visit us he would phone us up first so that we could be standing by the door to let him in. Anybody else who visited us came to the door and rang the bell. We had our own little secret alarm switch by the door so that when we peeped through the spy hole to see who the visitor was, we could warn everyone in the bay by our little alarm if the visitor was of some importance. If so, we would all race around, hiding our gash jobs from view, turning on all of our valve driven (but then high tech) test sets and giving the immediate impression of 'noses to the grindstone'.

Butch and I had this worked out to a tee, we had to really, as the visitor came into our bay first on his way to the office to talk to 'Masserati'. (He was actually called Mick Asserati, so was called 'Masserati' for short.) Anyway, Butch would immediately start to polish a set of propellers (polished props meant that the torp travelled faster through the water) on the good old rag wheel, using jeweller's rouge (we had a few spare sets of props that needed to be polished for the next month's quota of work anyway) and I would be fitting or removing (depending on whether I had fitted or removed it the last time someone came to the door) a primary battery or something that had spent the last two weeks in the half in/half out position. If the zobbits (the officer corps) knew what was going on they never let on and could do nothing about it anyway. I don't think that they ever knew; I have said before that they are very easy meat when it comes to pulling wool over eyes.

Anyway, my compadre, Butch, was a real craftsman and in his spare time he used to manufacture made-to-measure shotgun stocks for the local populace, using tools that he had made from hacksaw blades and the like. When he was due to leave the RAF, he sent a sample of his work to Purdy's, that rather well known gun maker, and they offered him a job. He made up his mind that if he was good enough to be offered a job by Purdy's then he would emigrate to Canada and set up a business there. He did eventually emigrate with his family but that was the last I heard from him apart from a postcard he sent me from on board the ship.

Butch had a wife called Maisie. Now Butch was only about 5 ft 2 inches tall and his wife was about six foot. I once asked him why he had married someone so tall and he said that she was the only woman that he had been able to screw and suck her nipples at the same time.

Butch and Maisie had a strange relationship. He would often drive past her in his little Ford Thames van and would not stop to give her a lift, even though their married quarter was quite a way from the village of Limavady and hence the entrance to the camp, which was in the middle of the village. He gave me a lift home once at lunchtime and we saw Maisie pushing the pushchair up the hill having just walked out of Limavady. He drove past and just waved at her. I said 'Aren't you going to stop and give her a lift?' He said 'No, let the bitch walk. I suppose this means I will have to wait for my dinner now.' Strange behaviour, but it didn't seem to bother either of them.

He had apparently first met Maisie in Singapore at a party (she was a WRAF) and he said that he liked the look of her when she, and the other girls, played the river game. Because Singapore was so hot and humid, many of the girls did not wear knickers under their long, thin, loose skirts. Under-skirts were definitely taboo also. During parties, the boys used to blindfold all the girls and tell them that they were going to play the river game. After the girls were blindfolded the boys would put mirrors around the floor and they would then lead the girls through the room and told them that they had to step over the river, which was in fact, the mirror. All the boys were, obviously, peering into the mirrors to see who was and who was not wearing knickers. The girls who did not wear the knickers were, for some strange reason, the most popular that night. Out of the few girls who would not play 'the river game', some were either a waste of time or were just suffering from that well known female ailment that they suffer from every 28 days or so.

The girls claimed that they never actually knew why the boys played this strange game, but somehow I don't believe that, they knew what the purpose was.

Some of our other activities at BK included torpedo drops. Out of the three Torp Bays in UK we were the only ones to drop any exercise ones, and then it was only the Mk 44, as enough info had been gleaned on the old Mk 30 over the years.

I used to look after the exercise head that replaced the warhead. The head consisted of loads of sensors that provided the recorder with information on what the torp was doing. Things like speed, depth, single or double pulse acoustics (the 'ping' that all the submarine films use), elevator and rudder positions, battery power, signal response etc. About 20 different torp activities were recorded as exposed lines or blips etc. on a camera film about 125 feet long and 4 inches wide. At the end of its run, the exercise head would blow a little squib (small explosive charge) to dump a lead weight, which in turn had been retaining a load of lead shot. With all the lead fitted, the torp was negatively buoyant (i.e. it sank) but when the lead was dumped the torp became positively buoyant and, unless the torp had leaked water a bit, it would then float to the surface, perhaps from 1000 ft down.

One particular time we were on the usual Air-Sea Rescue boat from Portrush to pick up the torps that had been dropped by the Shack in the same bit of the Irish Sea that the Royal Navy (fish-heads) submarine 'target' boat had been sent to 'lurk'. The sub had reported that this particular torp had chased it like a terrier with a rat and the sub had classed themselves as duly sunk.

At the end of its run we stooged around looking for the 'day-glo' painted nose of the torp to pop its head out of the water. This did not happen but we did eventually spot it just a few feet under the water. We tried everything that we could to recover that torp but we just couldn't get it. Butch was all for diving in and trying to push it up to the surface but as this was about February time it would have been a bit foolhardy. We tried to get it out for hours but in the end it just slowly sank. Very frustrating! Ah well, one film less for Butch and me to develop.

We used to develop the film in our little battery room that was about 6 ft square. We sealed it off from the light, installed the safety light and off we would go. The high tech kit that we used to develop this 125 ft of film that had cost the use of an aircraft, submarine, recovery boat, lots of personnel and time, consisted of a tin bucket of developer and the same of fixer. The Photo Section on camp refused to do the developing without the correct kit (wimps!) so we did it as best we could. We got quite adept at winding the film through the relevant solutions loosely through our fingers from one end to the other and back again for the correct amount of time. At the end of all this we then had between four and ten rolls of film hanging all over the storage racks to dry.

We also became experts at interpreting the film, which to the untrained eye just consisted of loads of squiggly lines, dots and dashes across the width of the film, which continued in a haphazard fashion for the whole length of the film. The air-crew could not make head nor tail of the films so interpretation was left to us and we had to write a second by second account of what the torp actually did.

This meant that we were able to spot the mistakes that the air-crew had made. This they definitely did not like. When they are up there they are virtually answerable to no-one; who knows what switches they select. All air-crew, especially single-seat or twin-seat aircraft, do not like to be shown that they have done something wrong with their aeroplane, especially when we peasants, the ground-crew, are looking. Anyway, it has always been said that flying aeroplanes must be easy or the air-crew would make us engineers do it.

The carrier bay had the same problem with the Nuclear Depth Charge Carrier. Whenever the air-crew were simulating using the nuke, a response simulator was fitted to the carrier. This was removed at the end of the flight and sent off to the Carrier Bay to be interrogated. As this often proved that the air-crew had 'finger trouble' by indicating incorrect switch selection, the interrogator was taken away from the ground-crew and locked up in 'Ops' so that only the air-crew ever got to see it.

Still, we ground-crew were not always perfect. I remember one day when I was wandering from the Carrier Bay back to the Torpy Bay, a tractor from the bomb dump came tearing past me at a great rate of knots. Bearing in mind that he was towing a trolley behind him he was definitely going too fast. As he passed me a practice bomb fell off the trolley and landed at my feet.

Practice bombs in those days were those nasty 25 lb things filled with Titanium Tetrachloride, which was pretty revolting stuff. Filling the practice bombs in the winter with TitTet (as it was known) was a particularly onerous task. Apart from the fact that the task had to be done in a so-called 'building' that was more akin to a tube, with the open ends facing into the prevailing wind to blow any accumulated fumes away, and wearing rubber everything, it burned on contact with the air and gave off a great profusion of toxic smoke.

Anyway, back to the bomb that fell off the trolley. As the bomb fell the plastic tail section cracked and broke open, revealing all the nasty stuff.

Naturally, as a good armourer, I leapt out of the way. I looked behind me and realised that a trail of smoking bombs had been scattered all the way from the bomb dump gates. Looking forward again I realised that the smoking trail continued up the road. My shouting did no good at all and that guy was on his way to the Squadrons. Of course, when the ground-crew do something wrong it is easily spotted so he was hung, drawn and quartered.

He was only trying to rush for the benefit of the service and if he had driven at the correct speed then the air-crew would have moaned like pie-ards, 'cos they would not have had any toys to play with.

We were not the only people to break the rules; at least we break the rules to try to benefit the smooth running of the service.

The previous occupants of BK during the war, i.e. the yanks, didn't have a care in the world and were very sloppy. When they left at the end of the war, they just buried tons of ammunition inside the bomb dump. Some 25 years later some building work was being done in the dump, when the JCB scooped up a few buckets of soil to reveal tons of 20 mm ammunition buried just below the surface.

Wonderful people!

Whilst at BK my first son Mark was born in Limavady Cottage hospital in the middle of the night. In those days the menfolk were not allowed to be with their wives during labour. A lot of hospitals on the mainland had started to allow husbands to be present but this was definitely taboo in Northern Ireland. Me! Now where was I during the birth of my son? Ah yes, I remember, I was fast asleep in our married quarter at 14, Fort Drive.

There did not seem to be a lot of point in both 'wifey' and me being awake, so there I was, fast asleep whilst my wife was in labour. I suppose some of you will be thinking 'selfish pig', but you have to remember that things were different in those days and when I rang during the evening of labour the Irish nurse told me to go to bed and sleep, so I did just that so I did.

After Mark was born and I used to go and visit them, 'Wifey' would pass me the day's issue of Guinness. Very civilised the Irish; mums were given a bottle of Guinness a day by the hospital all on the bill of the National Health. 'Wifey' didn't drink at all so she used to give the bottle to me. A grand lass!

We used to drive north out of Northern Ireland into Southern Ireland to a place called Buncrana. If you think that driving north to travel from north to south of any island could only happen in Ireland, you would be right; check the map if you don't believe me. Anyway, the main reason to travel to Buncrana, apart from the fact that it was a day out at the seaside, was that draught Guinness was only 1/6d (7 ½ pence) a pint and it was nectar, smooth as silk. We were soon to learn that the Irish consider that Guinness does not like travelling and this particular brew was made just up the road. 'Bootiful', as Bernard Mathews would say.

It was at BK that I was promoted to Sergeant. This was it, a member of the most exclusive club in the world, the 'Sergeants' Mess'. The Officers like to think that they have the most exclusive club, but that is not true. Their mess has the local mayor, chief of police and other 'hangers on' (sorry, local dignitaries!) who all manage to become members and treat it like their own private club, which of course it is. After-hours drinking and other activities that would involve a public licensee losing his licence, are all done legally in the messes, as the 'law of the land', at least as far as little things like drinking hours and liquor licences are concerned, does not apply to military bases. Obviously, this also applies to the Sergeants' Mess, so we get the same benefits, except that members of our mess had to be a 'sneck' or ex sneck or a civil servant working with us and of the same relative rank, but apart from that, no scroungers.

At BK we had four squadrons of Shacks; 201, 203, 204 and 210 as well as the ASWDU (Anti-Submarine Warfare Development Unit) pronounced 'as-wer-doo'.

The gods upon high decided that one of the Squadrons had to be posted to Malta and the chosen one was 203. Of course this meant a scramble and lots of jockeying for position depending on whether individuals wanted to go to Malta or not.

The Irish lads on 203 obviously did not want to go, so they tried to make swaps with lads on other Squadrons who did want to go. Some others in Engineering Wing who were desperate to get away from Ulster were trying to get onto the squadron as a means of escape. Most of the air-crew were anxious to get away from BK as it was not a favourite place with them to fly from.

At the end of the runway was this huge mountain with a sheer face. Take off meant that as soon as the aircraft thundered down the runway and lifted its wheels from the floor then a hard turn was required to miss the cliff face. The mountain itself was called 'Ben Twitch' for obvious reasons. Moreover, due to the amount of rain that Ulster was 'blessed' with, we always had a saying that if you could not see Ben Twitch, it was raining, and if you could see Ben Twitch, it was about to rain. The runway was always wet and slippery through a combination of perpetual rain and the fact that the airfield was actually below sea level and only prevented from flooding by the 24-hour operation of a land drainage pump, that always seemed to be breaking down.

We had quite a few Shacks slide off the runway and into the quagmire that was the airfield. They were classed as Category 3 (Repairable) when assessed just after they slipped in, but were usually Cat 5 (Scrap) by the time that we managed to dig them out after they had sunk up to the wings. Yes, the undercarriage was down!

A number of second line people would also be going to Malta and as torps were to be transferred, they wanted to send a couple of torp trained and experienced lads out. I volunteered (after first discussing it with 'wifey' of course, what do you take me for? However, if she had said that she didn't want to go then I would have volunteered anyway, and then told her that 'those swines of posters people have posted me anyway'), along with one of the Chiefs, and we were duly selected.

It was obviously time to leave Northern Ireland anyway, as the Apprentice Boys of Derry were starting their tricks. The troubles in Ulster were started for a number of reasons but mainly because of the 'one man one vote' argument. Apparently, most of the Protestant folk had more than one vote but things were different for the Catholic (Republican) voters. Apparently, some of the Catholic voters had no vote at all. All of the Republican grumbles were allowed to be brought to the surface due to the fact that the British Government disbanded the 'B Specials'. Just in case any of you don't know, the 'B Specials' were a fully authorised Protestant secret police organisation that kept the peace in Ulster. A few people were killed by their guns, but only one or two per year!!! The main thing is that they did keep the peace and since their

65

disbandment, thousands have died. Anyway, as the IRA started to use their newly found freedom to make trouble, we flew off to Malta.

THE FAMOUS SHACKLETON SONG

Shackletons Don't Bother Me.

Assemble people as four engines and starter crew)

Give me a 3 (make noise like first engine starting and continue)
Give me a 4 (make noise like second engine starting and continue)
Give me a 2 (make noise like third engine starting and continue)
Give me a 1 (Make noise like fourth engine starting and continue)
(Continue making coughing and spluttering noises just like real Shack
   engines, all the way through the remainder of the song)
Shackletons don't bother me,
Shackletons don't bother me,
Clapped out abortions with flaps on their wings,
F*** all their pistons and their piston rings,
For we're saying goodbye to them all,
3/5s and 5/8s of f*** all,
You'll get no enjoyment
On coastal employment
So cheer up my lads bless 'em all.
Now they say that the shack is a mighty fine kite,
This we no longer doubt,
When you're in the air
With a Mig on your tail
This is the way to get out.
Keep calm and sedate mate,
Don't let your British blood boil,
Don't hesitate, slam it straight through the gate
And smother the B****** in oil.
Singing Shine Somerset Shine
The skipper looks on us with pride,
He'd have a blue fit
If he saw all the shit
on the side of the Somerset Shine.
This is my story, this is my song,
I've been in this Air Force too bloody long,
So roll on the Rodney, Repulse and Renown
You sank the Hood 'cause the bastard's gone down,
Chocks away, hashanay,

We'll chase all the Snowdrops that come down our way,
And their wives and their daughters for their bloody lives
Now there is a moral to our little song
If we all stick together we just can't go wrong,
So cheer up my lads, we'll sing it again
'cos we're Shackleton bombers off flying again.

7

RAF LUQA

(Torpedoes in the sun)

Off we flew in a Bristol Britannia, direct from BK to Malta; all three of us.

Now that in itself was an unusual thing for an overseas posting. The normal way was for the husband to fly out first, find accommodation, either private or if you had enough points then either a quarter or hiring. (A hiring is a private house that the RAF rents from a local landlord and then rents to the serviceman just like a quarter.) There were very few quarters in Malta and they were already occupied by the folk who had already started their tours.

More hirings were being taken on but that was a slow process. A fact that annoyed us immensely was that they were being allocated to the squadron guys whose effective date of posting was six weeks before they actually arrived on the island.

The second line guys, of whom I was one, only started their way up the housing list with effect from their posting date, which was the day that they landed in Malta. We didn't know this as nobody had bothered to tell us mere mortals these things. The end result of course was that all of the squadron guys were moved straight into hirings, which were far better accommodation, and all the second line guys had to scrape around for somewhere to live.

Our particular aircraft was full of families, who I recognised as being mostly from second line at BK and therefore destined to be second line at Malta. Upon landing at RAF Luqa the few squadron guys, with their families, were taken straight out to their allocated hiring and left to 'March In'. We, on the other hand, were now given the griff and informed of this wonderful plan that the families office people had dreamed up. We were herded onto a row of buses and driven round the island, stopping at various sites of private accommodation, which were mostly flats. We were shown around these infested 'dumps' and told to speak up if we wanted to live in any of them.

By the end of the first four hours, not one family had offered to live in any of them.

We were informed that as the day went on the accommodation would get worse. 'Worse!' Impossible.

By this time, everyone started to get somewhat concerned. The rents were high, the accommodation grim, the kids were getting agitated, wives were starting to get angry and the poor serviceman was told that he had to choose something before the end of the day, otherwise they would just be allocated the pig-sty that they were expected to live in.

The RAF has never had any clue on how to look after its people properly; even the grunts are looked after ten times better than we ever were. It was always said that the services looked after their priorities in descending order. In the case of the 'grunts', it was first and foremost 'the squaddie' who was top of the pile; the fishheads looked after the ship and its crew equally; but the Air Force looked after the aircraft, then aircrew, then officers and somewhere further down the list were we poor erks.

My wife and I had a quick 'conflab' (discussion) and decided that we would go for the little rabbit hutch that we had just seen in Birzibugga. At least it was on the coast road and because it was a flat on the second floor we were overlooking the sea. And whilst it was on the second floor, the building only had two floors anyway so we also had the roof that we could go on when the sun shone. We were looking forward to some sunshine (we had arrived in January, not warm enough to sit in the sun), which Malta is famous for; far better than the perpetual rain that Ireland is famous for.

So there we were, plonked in a grubby little flat with one and a half bedrooms, a tiny kitchen, with a tiny lounge that was overlooking the sea, in a strange town and in a strange country with nothing but the suitcases that we had carried out with us and the pushchair for Mark.

Our first priority was to find food for ourselves and Mark and by now it was starting to get dark. Lucky for us, the shops in Malta close for siesta round about 1400 hrs (2 pm to you civvies) and open up again for the evening at about 1700 hrs (work it out for yourselves). We managed to find a little shop that sold some food and another that sold the few necessities that were required (like toilet paper and light bulbs etc.) as the flat was virtually devoid of anything that we considered necessary to support life, apart from two pans, two plates, two bowls, two cups and saucers and a very meagre supply of furniture.

We even managed to buy and sampled the local vino, well at least I did, my wife was not into any form of alcohol. All alcohol was very cheap in Malta, a bottle of wine cost something like 10d. (4p) per bottle. Even then we would get a 1d return on the bottle. Anyway, after some food and wine we eventually settled down for the night.

The next day, luckily, was a Saturday. Saturdays meant no work then. We were thankful for that as it gave us a bit of time to find our bearings and get ourselves sorted out a bit. After Mark had been born, my wife had proved herself a very capable wife and mother and had then settled into the routine of service life. After we had been dumped in Malta she soon had our little flat ship-shape and we knew that the deep sea boxes, full of our belongings, were not too far behind us as we had sent them on ahead of us by about eight weeks.

During our wanderings around 'Birzy' we met other people who we had seen on the plane and exchanged horror stories. It transpired that we were quite lucky, as a lot of the flats had been infested with rats, cockroaches, ants and various other beasts. We had a few cockroaches (who didn't in Malta!) but we used to buy various powders which at least kept some of them at bay, and we were issued with a large can of DDT spray per week, which saw off some of the other bugs. (The DDT will probably end up killing us prematurely but we did not know that at the time; I wonder if the MoD knew, maybe we could all sue them!)

The Monday morning found quite a few of us at various points in the streets, standing around in our KD (Khaki Drill) with our protruding sickly white skin bits of legs, arms and heads, looking for something that resembled an RAF bus.

Sure enough, an old 'baked bean can' (so called 'cos they looked like they had been made out of second hand baked bean tins; just a sparse tin bus with the barest of interiors) duly arrived and picked us all up and drove us all off to RAF Luqa which was about 7 or 8 miles away.

At Luqa we did the customary 'arrivals' procedure with the famous blue card. This meant all of us traipsing around camp trying to find all the places that needed to know of our arrival so that someone could sign the card, certifying that note had been made of our presence. I went in to see my new boss who promptly informed me that I was to work in the Ejection Seat Bay.

Funny, thinks I, they must have carried out a pretty swift modification to the Torps to make them into one man submarines with ejection seats. My mind wandered to envisage the scene:

The Shack seeks out the enemy submarine using its sonobuoys.

Shack opens its bomb bay doors and releases a torpedo.

The torp comes down on its parachute with an ejection seat bolted to the middle and a frogman pilot sitting in the seat with reins attached to the rudders and foot pedals for the elevators.

When the torp enters the water, the pilot steers the torp to the enemy sub.

Just before the torp hits the sub to blow it to smithereens, the frogman pilot ejects and the seat sends him through the water, into the air to be scooped up by the Shack and flown back to base. My Hero! Brilliant.

Just as I was musing on this top secret development, the boss told me that no-one had told him that torp trained and experienced men were coming out so he had sent some of his men back to UK to do the torpedo course and then installed them into the torp bay to run it. My job was to fill a post left vacant by a guy who was now working in the torp bay, i.e. the Ejection Seat Bay that maintained the seats of Canberra PR9 recce aircraft. Typical RAF organisation!

After the first few days the RAF stopped sending buses for us as it expected us to get ourselves sorted out with a car. This was no easy task as the cars on the island were mostly of pre-war vintage and the 'Malts' tended to keep a car for life.

Any of the guys who did manage to get a second hand car used to spend on average something like two hours per day on maintenance trying to keep them going. My mate Ron Moss had an old Austin 12 and he definitely spent more than two hours per day looking after and tinkering with that.

As soon as anyone got a car they immediately used to fill it up with passengers giving them lifts into work. I opted to buy a brand new car and decided on that chic little machine called the Singer Chamois (a fancy version of the Hillman Imp).

I have always liked port wine, and I soon discovered that by mixing various red wines with the very cheap sugar (it was on ration) and even cheaper brandy, I could make a very palatable port. Just for anyone who does not know, both port and sherry are made from the same ingredients. The difference being that port has the brandy added (adding the brandy is why port and sherry are called 'fortified' wines) after fermentation and sherry has the brandy added before fermentation.

I suppose my early experiments with these concoctions persuaded me that it was not a good idea to buy a car straight away. I could get lifts in to work and the local Maltese bus company provided a good service, which was both regular and cheap. The buses used in Malta were also pre-war; but in this case I think they were pre First World War. They had no signs on them that said where they were going to. They used to be colour coded with different colour bands around the middle. Virtually every bus went to and from the capital, Valletta. The buses on the Birzy run had bands that were coloured blue and yellow (yellow, blue, yellow, I think). Simple really once you knew the score.

Most people bought a new car eventually but they had to be ordered and shipped from the UK and took about three months to arrive. The car that I ordered was, as I said earlier, a Singer Chamois and, as we could buy them duty free, it cost me the grand total of £535 on the road.

The arrival of the car meant that we could get off to visit the few beaches that the island is blessed with, which were mostly at the top of the island. Birzy was at the bottom.

At least we had Kalafrana down at our end, which was the old sea-plane base during the war. The kids could go down the slipways and paddle whilst everybody else who could swim did so from the concrete or rocks.

Work in the seat bay was uneventful but I did get myself a detachment to an Italian air base at Treviso not far from Venice. The Canberras were doing a photo mapping job for the Italian Government and we were sent up to keep the old girls flying. As my job was primarily to do seat independent checks, there was not a lot to do. In any case, the aircraft were only flying in the mornings, due to the build up of haze in the afternoons. This meant that most afternoons were free.

The Italian Air Force were wonderful. They provided us with a proper bus, which was an 'eyetie' airforce bus, with curtains and real seats, just like civvy buses. The only difference appeared to be that every time the driver changed gear it seemed that he had three gearboxes and three gear levers to juggle. Good job we didn't have to provide our own driver, which was mostly what we had to do if someone loaned us a bus.

It seems that only our Air Force is so stingy with anything to do with creature comforts, at least as far as ground-crew are concerned. Even the Italian conscripts were strutting around in what looked like generals' uniforms, covered in 'gold' insignia up their arms and down their chests, whilst we were still wearing 'Hairy Marys'.

Anyway, the bus driver said that we could go anywhere we wanted to, so we did the grand tour. Up the mountains to Cortina to look at the ski jump, couple of times to Venice, Turin and the other big towns. We all had a great time. Some of the lads even had their wicked way with an Italian girl, but not many; and not me. Just for a change, I was a good lad.

We had a few Canberras crash whilst I was in the seat bay. The seats all worked 'as advertised' but four air-crew were killed. A couple when they ejected, and the aircraft was too low to the ground and the sink rate too high, and another couple when the aircraft was again too low to the ground and also upside down during ejection.

It is a trying time for the ejection seat bay lads when any aircraft crashes, as there is a medical team at the IAM (Institute of Aviation Medicine) based at Farnborough who research every crash to make sure that the seat performed as it should. For this reason, and the fact that the lads in seat bays are very conscientious anyway, ejection seat maintenance is the most meticulous of all equipment maintenance.

This brings out the maxims; 'When all else fails, the seat must work' and 'If in doubt, throw it out' (when examining a component part) and similar little well known sayings and phrases. These words could be seen pasted up on the wall of many ejection seat bays and is ingrained into the heart of all armourers.

I managed to get out of the seat bay and into the carrier bay at about the same time that we were provided with a hiring. My time in the carrier bay was again uneventful but that almost wasn't the case. I was working on a Light Store Carrier and the guy next to me was testing a mini-crate that had just been returned from the Canberra Squadron.

Everybody knows that a gun is always checked to make sure that it is unloaded as soon as it passes into their hands. Well a mini-crate is a bit like a whole collection of guns all tied together and which hold a number of photo flash cartridges that fired a charge out of the Canberra bomb bay at great force which after a short delay of about one second, exploded and burned at umpteen million candle power so that the aircraft could take happy snaps at night. (Yes, just like a flash-gun that all you 'clickers' (photographers) know, but in this case, it was like the flash-gun was thrown out of the aircraft first!)

As the guy was about to run the test the 'Chief' came wandering through and asked the inevitable question. 'Have you checked to ensure that that mini-crate is not loaded in accordance with AP whatever'? (He didn't really say that, he actually said something like 'I hope you've checked that bloody thing hasn't got any carts left in it, you idiot', but things like that are never said in a book are they? It is just like in the 1930s films where they say things like 'Take this you bounder (biff)' and 'Darling, will you miss me terribly??' etc. You get the idea.)

I don't really know why I should bother telling you the rest 'cos by now it should be fairly obvious what I am going to say.

No, he hadn't checked to ensure no cartridges were fitted, and yes, it did have a cartridge in, and yes, the test would have fired the cartridge, and yes, it would have dissolved our feet and ankles and blinded us to boot.

The next hiring was in Gzira and was a downstairs flat with the owner living upstairs. It was a lot bigger than our little matchbox in Birzy. Also by now, my wife was pregnant again.

I used to get home from work in the early afternoon and take Mark for walks whilst my wife had a break and an afternoon nap. I didn't realise at the time how much bonding took place between Mark and me during those walks around deserted Gzira (it was siesta time). We used to chase 'chit-chats' (little lizards), both real and imaginary, through the streets. Mark once picked up a feather and put it in a matchbox and said that it was his pet 'chit-chat'. He kept that 'pet' for months.

Our evening entertainment during the week consisted of mostly playing cards with Pete and Veronica, who were in a flat in the block next door to us. They were fanatical about Canasta so we spent many a happy hour learning the multitude of rules and playing the game.

Pete had an old Rover 75, the type with running boards, which was immaculate and very reliable. He was one of the few not to need to spend the two hours per day on maintenance and repairs.

By now I had managed to get myself back into the Torpy Bay. Back to doing the old 'systems test' and 'deck tests' on the Mk 44. At about the same time, our second son was born in the RN Hospital on the island, but his birth was actually registered in Cyprus, or I should say that he was registered at the Sovereign Base Area in Cyprus, which gave him UK citizenship automatically. Sometimes, someone forgot to register in Cyprus, which caused problems with immigration upon return to the UK. Questions were asked along the lines of 'Where did you get this foreign baby from'? He also had a Maltese birth certificate so he has the option of dual nationality should he ever be potty enough to want to be a Maltezer.

We duly had him christened 'Lee David', and it soon became apparent that he was a completely different character to Mark. Whereas we 'didn't know we had Mark' we soon realised that Lee was there. He ate everything put in front of him, including bread and jam at 13 weeks old. My wife used to feed him with a spoon in each hand, i.e. two spoons, for as soon as he got one spoonful into his mouth he screamed for the next. He was stubborn, demanding, noisy, etc. etc.

My wife always said that if Lee had been the first, there wouldn't have been a second.

We did not stay long in Gzira as we got the flat condemned. Every time that it rained, which luckily wasn't often and then only in the rainy season, the water came pouring down the inside wall and into the light switches and wall sockets. It then soon flooded the whole of the floor downstairs (remember we had a ground floor flat) so we ended up trying to squeegee it all out of the back door onto the patio. Now the patio had a wall all the way around it and drainage was via a pipe under the floor of the flat and out to the front of the property. We ended up with a swimming pool (I exaggerate slightly, it was more like the depth of a paddling pool) at the back of the flat with the interior of the flat flooded as well. It took quite a while to convince the families office that this was happening, but they eventually believed us and moved us out to another flat in Mtarfa.

This was now much better. The best job; the best hiring; two big pay rises given to us by a Labour Government no less; my wife happy and contented; Mark off to nursery school each morning with the nuns, who used to call him 'Baby Jesus' and treated him as such; Lee still as demanding as ever, but getting bigger and easier to cope with; more visits to the beach and the mess than ever before. Yes, things were looking pretty good for the last 18 months of our tour.

Soon after I joined the Torpy Bay, the updating of the RAF's weapon stocks had been completed and rumour had it that the RAF was storing something like a million tons of explosives on the island.

We had lots of explosive storage space, especially at Fort Mosta, but eventually, the time came for us to get rid of some of the old stock. The plan was made that we would deep-sea dump (we could do that with impunity in those days) quantity one thousand by 1000 lb bombs and quantity eight hundred by 8 in photo-flashes. It was decided to do this at night so as not to upset the locals, or to let them see what was going on. The stores were all first moved to Kalafrana, the old sea-plane unit down Birzy way, and then by lighter to a ship.

Needless to say, the Russian fishing boats, the ones with all the aerials around them and with other funny looking fishing gear, suddenly decided that all the fish in the world were now just offshore from Kalafrana.

When we had eventually loaded everything onboard our ship, it upped anchor and made a beeline to Israel at a slow speed. Israel had, at this time, just had their first proper 'punch up' with their Arab neighbours. The ship was soon followed by most of the Russian fleet that was based in the Med, only to find that our ship veered off at the very last minute and started to dump its explosives. The games that nations play!

We were living close to our friends Ron and Maisie Moss and spent quite a deal of time with them and various other neighbours. Trips to the beach and other social events sometimes took place 'en masse'. At the mess on a Saturday night, the first part of the evening entertainment consisted of bingo, which was then followed by the Saturday night hop.

Neither Ron nor I could stand bingo but our respective spouses loved it! I seem to recall that even some of the quite intelligent Snecks and Warrant Officers used to like 'playing' it. No accounting for taste is there!

Anyway, Ron and I would take our spouses in either his or my car to the mess, drop them off to play their Bingo, and we would then drive off into Valletta and go to the pictures. At the end of the film we would drive back to the mess and by that time the dreaded bingo would be just finishing and the mess hop would begin. This was a very civil arrangement. If the film finished early we would have a few beers in the city first and then drive back to base.

I remember one of our circle was Ann with the long blonde hair. She was married to a store-man but apart from that she was quite sane and she was very attractive. She let it be known to me that she fancied me, but apart from a kiss and a bit more than a cuddle once, we never had the opportunity to go the whole way. Soon after that her hubby got posted to the store-man's graveyard (16 MU Stafford), so that was the end of that. It did make me realise that I certainly still fancied the ladies!

When I first got into the Torpy bay, it was run by a little chief called Ron (not my mate Ron, he was an engine fitter on 203 Sqdn). He was soon posted and the bay then consisted of three sergeants. As I was the senior I was made 'iccy' (in charge).

Soon after this, the boss called me over (his office was on the other side of the airfield) to see him and he told me that our bay was about to be taken over by the US company that built the Mk 44 torpedo. It transpired that they were trying to sell the Mk 44 torp to a far eastern navy and a demonstration had to be laid on for them. We were instructed to give them all assistance for the duration, which was scheduled to take 5 weeks. We were not to do any scheduled maintenance during this time and our sole purpose was to assist. The company people provided a list of their personnel; 12 engineers and a secretary, made up of qty 12 males and qty 1 female.

Well, it seemed obvious to us who was who, so it came as quite a surprise when the female asked me where she could work to set up the area for the torps recording head and one of the 'chaps' was running around with pencil and paper. A woman doing engineering work; whatever next? If I had a moustache it would definitely have twitched. Women didn't do that sort of thing, or at least they didn't in 1970!

As I had worked on the recorder head at BK I gave her (Janet her name was) a hand and we got on famously and became quite friendly!

It soon became apparent that neither the company nor the MoD had thought of the film development and neither had the girl. (She wasn't all that brilliant!) When I mentioned it to her, her face dropped a mile and she raced off to see the company top man. He came in with a worried look on his face and asked if I knew of anyone on the island who could develop the film. I explained about Butch and me at BK and a great smile of relief came over his face.

We set up the dark room in our battery bay and after the first drop I showed my compadre Pete how to do the 'biz' and we developed the film, hung it out to dry and then interrogated it just like we had done at BK.

The run had been a total failure. The torp hadn't even started its dive, it had just gone down to ISD. (Initial search depth, something that was set by the aircrew when the sonobuoy told them how deep the sub was.) The Navy man was due to arrive at any time so, after a quick word with the company boss and our own boss, we hid the film, exposed a blank to the light, quick develop and fix, ran it up and down the bay to dry it out until the guard on the bomb dump gate rang us to say that the Navy man was on his way. The Torpedo facilities were all located within the bomb dump, more correctly referred to as the ESA (Explosive Storage Area) so we were completely surrounded by barbed wire and guarded 24 hours per day. Anyway, The far eastern chap took our story that the film was a failure but the torp was probably OK. Foreign navy officers are as easy to hoodwink as our own!

The navy did buy the torp in the end but only after a few failures that had to be re-run. The company stayed for 15 weeks altogether and during that time they took us, and our wives, to all the best places on the Island. My wife had her first little gamble on the roulette; just a couple of pounds, but it was something that she had always wanted to do.

Just before they left, Janet asked me if I would show her the torpedo facilities, so I showed her the components storage buildings, ready-use storage, battery storage, acid storage and last on the list was the weapon prep room. I was explaining all about torpedo preparation when she locked the door from the inside and I soon realised that her interest in torpedo recorder heads also extended to 'head' of a different type. She was obviously thanking me properly, in that inimitable way that only a woman can, for saving her bacon for forgetting all about film developing.

Well, she hadn't seen her husband for 15 weeks and said she was so grateful for everything that I had done for her that 'she would do this small thing for me'! What did she mean by 'small thing' though? Cheek!

By now I had been asked by the boss if I would extend my tour by an extra 3 months. As we were originally due home in January and would land in the UK in perhaps the worst weather of the year, I agreed. We decided that we would send our deep-sea boxes back to the UK late January and we would be travelling back in March. We were still contemplating our good fortune at returning at a better time of year, when the Maltese had an election. Dom Mintoff was duly elected and he started screaming 'Brits out'.

Once it was announced that we were actually going to leave, all pandemonium broke loose. As the fear was that the Libyans were going to take over our bases (it was the promise of Libyan money that spurred Mintoff on), and that they would move in before we left, all the bases took on a fortress stance.

All of the locally recruited RAF and Army personnel were sent home indefinitely. Transport aircraft were flying in laden with 30 mm HE/I (High Explosive/Incendiary) ammunition, for Lightning fighters to fly in to protect us, demolition explosives to destroy all the buildings as we left, and extra army grunts to protect us. The grunts soon set up their little 'gun-pits' all over the place. Our Shack and Canberra aircraft were dispersed to Cyprus, Sigonella and Gibraltar. Packing some kit and destroying other bits of kit were the order of the day.

All the wives were left to pack up the household goods. They could use all soft furnishings that we had been loaned with our quarter/hiring, i.e. all bedding, curtains, tablecloths, towels etc, as packing material. Most people used to keep their wooden packing cases from when they came out but any that hadn't had to scrounge their own. The Maltese civvy transport lorry duly turned up to pick up our boxes, and as they were carrying them out, my wife was still painting our address on the box and I was still nailing the lids down. At one stage I climbed on the lorry to finish off the nailing. After our boxes had gone, everyone was then warned to ensure that the Maltese transport lorry was bone fide, as the Maltese soon learned that if they had a lorry, all they had to do was turn up at a hiring, ask for the boxes and all the worldly possessions of the occupant were there for the taking. We later learned that this had happened to quite a few unfortunate people.

My wife and the boys flew home a few days later. Whilst Lee was really too big for a 'sky-cot', one was made available just in case he started to 'play up'. Luckily, he apparently spent most of the time asleep or being 'nursed' by the other women on the kite. Mark spent most of the flight back to UK in the cockpit talking to the pilots and they promised him most faithfully that when the Air Force had finished with this particular Bristol Britannia whispering giant (as they were nicknamed), then they would deliver it to Mark to play with in our back garden, just as he had asked them to. After four months in transit, every one of our boxes, thankfully, arrived back in UK safely.

The number of servicemen left to clear up slowly dwindled, as the fear of the Libyans moving in before we left receded, until it was mostly Armourers that remained.

We had our famous million tons of explosives to move. By the time that we had cleared the torps and equipment and emptied the small bomb dump at Luqa, there was still lots at Fort Mosta. Every available man was destined for Mosta. I was given a 5-ton lorry and two SACs. Neither of the SACs could even drive a car, so I was given a licence on the spot to drive the lorry. The long drive from Fort Mosta to Kalafrana, laden to the gunnels with explosives of all sorts (certainly a lot more than 5 tons) and the SACs riding shotgun, was without incident, even after the hundred or so times that we did it.

As the end came closer, my little team were sent to Safi to ensure that all the buildings had been emptied. I was given the keys to all the buildings and told that if anything had been left, it was to be smashed to pieces. My young SACs enjoyed that as it gave them a chance to vent their frustration. They really got stuck into wrecking the place, smashing windows, breaking down walls, putting cement down the toilets and sinks and reverse wiring the mains electrics so that everything would short out as soon as power was applied. This was, after all, what had been happening at all of the British military bases in Malta.

We came to a building that had been the car club. I opened it up and saw a cherry red Austin Healey Sprite Mk 1, the frog-eye variety. It was absolutely immaculate, concourse condition, apart from the fact that it had its cylinder head removed, which was lying on the bench at the side.

It was beautiful! We all looked at it in awe. How could we smash this beautiful machine that was obviously the apple of someone's eye? Our instructions were to smash anything left; why hadn't the owner managed to get it on the ship that was taking our cars home for free? I thought about trying to contact one of my Maltese colleagues or friends, but by this time, after all the families and most personnel had left, the few remaining had been withdrawn to 'live-in' at Luqa and we were not allowed any outside contact; trying to get hold of someone would not be possible and I had no time to do so anyway.

My thoughts went to Vick, a sergeant just posted out to the torp bay as the troubles were just starting. He had ordered his car, a Triumph Spitfire GT6, and the garage rang him to say that it was in the showroom ready to be picked up the day it was announced that we were getting out. He told the garage to hang on to it for a couple of days. The RAF then stated that all cars purchased on HP (hire purchase) had to be paid in full before they left the island and that interest free loans could be obtained from the MoD so that any outstanding loans could be paid, just for the asking. Then it was announced that the time factor for keeping a car on the island for more than a year to qualify for tax free import into the UK had been waived by Customs and Excise. Then it was announced that all cars would be transported back to the UK free.

Vick rang the garage, negotiated a new, lower, price for the car, told them to leave the wax on and he would pay in cash and pick it up the next day. He went to accounts, showed them his original paperwork with the old price on, signed for the money, took it (less the amount he had got reduced on the car) to the garage, drove the car straight down to the docks, peering through a small hole he had cleared in the windscreen wax and ended up with a brand new, tax free, car back in the UK that he paid for with an interest free loan. He then got posted back to the UK and drove that car around for the next 16 years. Some people came out pretty well!

But what about this cherry red Austin Healey frog-eye Sprite that sat in its bay, looking at us so mournfully.

The answer was, 'Nothing!'

None of us could do anything about it. I locked the building up again and went back and informed the 'powers that be' that Safi was now cleared. I thought that someone may get pleasure from it; some Maltese or even a Libyan or whatever, someone else would either love and cherish it or else they would 'smash up the accursed English car'. It would be up to them, my conscience was clear.

I eventually flew out of Malta halfway through my tour extension, having spent 6 weeks of my life living in mayhem. It was at that point that the RAF announced that they were going to return for a few more years. Oh dear! Rumour had it that it cost the British taxpayer £5M to get out of Malta and £12M to go back in again; I wonder why?

One of the young SACs in the bomb dump ended up in Sigonella, his wife in Gibraltar, his dog in Cyprus and his boxes containing all his belongings in some Maltese lorry driver's house, him having handed his boxes to a non-authorised lorry driver.

Some people came out of it not well at all! Oh well, such is life.

I was to be posted to somewhere that no-one in the RAF seemed to have ever heard of. I was told that I would be informed of where it was and a map of how to get there would be sent to me at my 'disembarkation address'. It all sounded very 'hush-hush'.

8

RAF OUSTON

(Northern England Travel Centre)

The great majority of the RAF never knew that RAF Ouston existed. I certainly didn't.

When I was told of my posting, even the people in the General Office at Luqa had no idea where it was or what was done there. Speculation abounded that it was a top-secret establishment and that I had been specially selected for a special job.

General Office found out that the place was just outside Newcastle-upon-Tyne and at the same time I received a letter from the families office at Ouston, informing me that a married quarter had already been allocated to me and would I please let them know when I would be arriving.

Now that was definitely different! A letter from a new unit, direct to me and not via the 'powers that be' at my current unit, and a married quarter already allocated for me. Wow! It must be a very important job for an empty quarter to be sitting waiting for me.

I had bought a VW camper van as soon as we returned to the UK as my wife had now 'grown up' a bit and decided that she might, after all, like to go camping, so long as it was high up inside the camper and not on the ground where she could be attacked by those 'man-eating' worms. We had expended all of our disembarkation leave, loaded the camper up with family and possessions and set off 'oop north' on the A1 and up to Newcastle.

We then followed the map that had been provided by Ouston, took the A69 to Heddon-on-the-Wall and turned onto the B6318. At this point my instructions informed me to keep a sharp look-out for the Ouston sign as it was not on the map. Reinforcement for my theory that this was a top secret establishment hidden at an unknown place in the wilds of Northumberland.

We spotted the very small sign for RAF Ouston, and followed the little lane to the end, where we discovered a RAF ghost town. It was definitely an RAF camp with a hangar, gate (permanently in the 'up' position, in fact it was held in the 'up' position by a huge great lock), flagpole fluttering with the RAF Ensign, and all the quarters and camp buildings cluttered together in a small group. I went into the Guard Room and announced my arrival to the young SAC sitting reading a paper.

'What happens at this place?' I ask.

'Haven't a clue,' answers the SAC.

'How many people are there here?' is my next question.

'38 in all from the CO down to me,' he answers.

'The plot thickens,' I muse. 'How many of those are armourers?'

He looks at the board on the wall and says 'Two Sgts and a chief, who work in the hole,' came the bored reply.

Ah! Down the hole, has to be a hush-hush job. Thinks I.

I wander into the SHQ (Station Headquarters) building trying to find someone. Eventually I come across a WO who turns out to be the Station Adjutant, Families Officer, OC Admin, OC Station Services, and OC anything else of an admin nature.

He phones the Station Commander (who was having his coffee in the Officers' Mess) who says that he will come straight back to greet me. (What! A senior officer leaving the mess immediately to come to greet me, a lowly sergeant?)

After a few minutes, the station master, who was obviously the Sqdn Ldr mentioned by the SAC in the guardroom, arrives, puts his arm around my shoulders and leads me into his office. 'Your work in Malta was considered so stressful that you have been sent here for a rest. You will like the job here and it is nice and easy.'

'But what am I going to do?' I plead.

'ATC Liaison,' he announces.

There followed a long and strained silence. Followed by an even longer and more strained silence.

Now I have experienced the feeling of shell shock!

I 'March In' to our married quarter and learn that my next-door neighbour was no other than the other Sgt Armourer on the unit.

My wife and I got ourselves settled in to our new quarter and had a nice cup of char, but my mind was only on my neighbour; I just had to go and see him to find out if my worst fears were founded.

After seeing him driving his 'Beetle' back to his quarter at tea time, I was impatient to go round and meet him. I gave him a little time to eat but my impatience to discover my fate got the better of me and I went round to find he had not yet finished his tea. It transpired that he was a Scots lad called Bert (Strange how 'Roberts' get called 'Bob' in England but 'Bert' in Scotland).

After the usual introductions, Bert informed me that our job was to travel around the Air Training Corps, the dreaded 'Space Cadets' units, every six months. The main purpose for this was to check up on security for their small arms, deliver them any ammo (.22 calibre) from their entitlement, ensure that they had been servicing the weapons correctly etc. etc. Additionally, we were to work at weekends to supervise the cadets on the range and to issue the arms and ammo for their use.

Bert said that the job was a doddle and it only entailed us actually being at work for, on average, 3 days per week. Bert had been doing the job for a few years and seemed to like the thought of an easy life. The 'Chief' was on his 'last tour posting' so was not interested and Bert had sorted the system so that in the main we did not do any night visits; we always went to get the keys for the cadets 'hut', ammo and small arms lock-up from the key holder during the day.

We had the whole of Northumberland, Cumberland, Westmoreland, County Durham and North Lancashire to cover; quite a large area. I seem to recall that we had something like 63 units to visit twice per year. Our vehicle to travel over the whole of the North of England was usually a mini-van (hardly a high security vehicle, bearing in mind that we were mostly carrying arms and ammo).

The system was well and truly 'sussed' as we used to travel to Cumberland in the Spring and Autumn (the best time of year up there) and stay for a week at a time at one of the 'Outward Bound' type places and 'do' the Cumberland and Westmoreland units. Similarly, we would be off to Blackpool for a week to 'do' the North Lancashire ones.

We were issued with a second 'Best Blue' uniform to wear so that when we had done 'our bit' and were looking around town to buy our apples (it was traditional to buy Granny Smith apples in every town we visited) the local yobbos would look at us and think to themselves 'Coo, don't they look smart. I think that I will rush on down to the recruiting office and sign on to join the RAF this very day.' I kid you not, that is what some of our Officer Corps really thought.

There are some distinct advantages to being on a tiny camp like Ouston. For a start, everybody knew each other. Two couples who lived next door to each other took things to the extreme when they started wife swapping and eventually swapped completely and lived with the 'wife next door' permanently. Strange pair of pairs really. One of the women was as ugly as sin, the proverbial 'back end of a bus' and the other one was a real slim, trim, dolly-bird that everybody fancied (including me). Still, no accounting for taste; the grass is greener . . . etc.

Another very definite advantage was that we did not have a Medical Officer. We had a civilian doctor contracted to come in and hold a surgery about three times a week, but this was only for the terminally ill. Everyone else went to see the Corporal Medic at any time, day or night, and we would wander over to the dispensary and get boxes full of pills or a gallon of medicine, whatever was required, to sort us out. The system worked very well and whilst it may have been expensive in medication it was very cheap in doctor's time. However, we, like everybody else, stocked up on pills and Gees Linctus etc.

As an aside, Gees Linctus has now been taken off the market as all the BDMs (Brain Dead Morons) that the country seems to be full of these days used to buy it in huge quantities to give them a 'high'. (It used to contain a hallucinating drug of some sort.) The fact that some used to kill themselves with it, would appear to me to be a bonus to the country.

I have already mentioned that I had bought a VW camper van. Now camper vans are quite large and obviously do not fit in a standard garage. I had a look around the station, which had lots of empty buildings not being used, when I espied the old Mortuary attached to which was the ambulance garage. I had a chat with the Station Master who agreed that I could rent out the garage for the same price as the standard garage rent; something like 50p per week. I opened up the garage for the first time that it had been opened in years, cleaned it all out and saw that there were pipes and radiators in the garage. Further rummaging around in the morgue revealed valves on the plumbing, which I duly opened, and 'Hey Presto'; I now had a centrally heated garage and workshop. What a bonus!

Another advantage was that the window in the kitchen of our married quarter looked over the sports field to the old 'Op's building (the hole in the ground). This building was the telephone exchange (as originally planned) and the rest of the building was the Armoury. When we were locked away in the Armoury doing our paperwork, servicing the weapons or playing cards (mostly it seemed to be playing cards), we used to go off for lunch and tea as normal. Come 12 Noon or 1700 hrs approximately, my wife would be looking out of the kitchen window and see me walk out of the hole and across the grass. At this point she started to put our food on the plate and it would be ready to eat the instant that I walked in. What a civilised existence!

After I had visited all of the units once (we always travelled in pairs due to the security need ???), the novelty wore off. This was not what I joined 'The Mob' for. After a quick chat with my wife, I volunteered for Germany. It was always easy to get posted to Germany as we had loads of bases there and, strangely enough, PMC (The 'posting people') could never get enough volunteers. I had also made the mistake of applying for a commission. Anything to get away from Ouston really!

I got called forward to attend an aptitude test, so I started to read all the right papers, like the *Telegraph* and the *Times*, took on a secondary duty and all the other things that 'mark one out to be of potential' (like saying 'one' instead of 'me' or 'you' or whatever).

Anyway, I was sent down to Henlow for my test and interviews (which I failed by the way; One was so disappointed in oneself don't you know!) and on the way back by train I was standing in the buffet car when I noticed a rather glamorous and very beautiful lady with a mane of long black hair. (I am a sucker for long hair, always have been, always will be! I reckon that it should be mandatory for all females to wear their hair long and their skirts short.) Anyway, this particular beauty was wearing dark sunglasses even though it was not sunny. As I studied her I thought that she may be a TV star or something.

At the time, I was reading the stocks and shares page of the *Telegraph* (I had picked up the paper in the carriage) as I had made a disastrous venture into shares. (Including British Leyland; need I say more!) I threw the paper on the table in disgust and the sunglasses girl asked if she could borrow it.

Of course, I said that she could. She looked at the same shares pages and she also put the paper down in a bit of a huff. I asked her if her shares were doing badly, which she agreed, and we started talking about shares. She took off her sunglasses and I saw that she was absolutely beautiful! She really was stunning and had that lovely soft Edinburgh accent.

I looked at her and said, 'I feel that I should recognize you; TV, adverts, films or something?'

She said that she was just a housewife and not famous, but was flattered that I should think so. We started talking more. It transpired that she was married with two children, her husband had just gone off to Africa on a teaching job and she had just been down to London to visit her brother.

She was on her way back to Edinburgh where she lived, but was going to stop off in Doncaster for a few days to visit her other brother. The children were apparently already ensconced in a boarding school somewhere. She would be flying out to Africa to join her husband in about three months' time.

To cut a long story short, we agreed that we would both get off the train at Doncaster and I would show her the town of 'Dirty Donny'.

We looked around the town, had a Chinese meal and then went to the pictures that evening.

At that point it was just like that 1945 film called *Brief Encounter* with Celia Johnson and Trevor Howard, except that it was Margaret and me, instead of Celia and Trevor. However, unlike in the film, we booked into a hotel and enjoyed a whole night of delicious and exquisite passion. I had never known a night like it; I did not know where I had got the energy from. Making love had never felt so wonderful. Notice that I said 'making love', and did not use some sordid expression like 'bonking' or 'screwing', or any other word or phrase that just meant illicit nookie.

The next morning we went our separate ways.

We had, the previous night, worked out a way to keep in touch with each other by post. I started a PO Box number in Newcastle that she used to write to, and I wrote to her in a way that I shall not divulge just in case her husband happens to be reading this and could put two and two together. (Not that he is likely to be reading this!)

From then on, things were never the same with my wife. Life and sex (it was by now no longer classed as lovemaking; never was, I had now discovered) with my wife was boring. This was the eight year point in our marriage, which bearing in mind the fact that I had spent one year in Bahrain, equated to the proverbial seven year itch.

When I got back to Ouston, the news had come through that I had been posted to Germany. This meant that I first had to undertake an eight weeks course at Coningsby to learn about the Phantom aircraft, Additionally, I had to do a nuclear weapons course at Wittering.

Whilst at Coningsby, Margaret and I arranged that she would get down to Doncaster for two weekends and I would visit my parents just outside 'Donny' at the same time. We met and the wonderful VW camper was a godsend. So, as it turns out, was the site on which we enjoyed our passion. At the time, it was a building site, but when the building was completed, I was amazed to discover that the site was now a new nunnery. The tales of passion that nunnery could tell!

However, Margaret and I were in love. She wanted to disappear off the face of humanity with me, suggesting that we could set up a love nest in a remote Scottish croft or on an island or something. She was all for leaving everything behind her. I, on the other hand, realised that as a serving member of the RAF, they would not be so forgiving about me deserting. It was tempting though.

When I got back to Ouston after my courses, my wife said that she would like to go, with the children, to spend a couple of weeks with her parents just before we went to Germany. Well yes, I thought that a brilliant idea as Edinburgh was just up the road from Newcastle, and Margaret was due to join her husband at about the same time that I would be travelling to Germany.

I started to 'live in' for the last couple of weeks, and the first night that my wife had gone, there was a dance on camp, which of course, I went to. Whilst there, I noticed a girl giving me the proverbial 'eye'.

We started chatting.

Now, I used to be the treasurer of the Families Club (we did not have the usual Sergeants' Mess or NAAFI Club) as I had now been promoted to the rank of Chief Technician. The Families Club was in the Sergeants' Mess building and as I was the treasurer, I had an office in one of the wings of the building that was otherwise empty.

That girl had a gorgeous body and oozed sex appeal as well as being very attractive. However, she did have a look about her that shouted 'I'm a slut'. We ended up in my office where I screwed her on my chair, on my desk, in the shower and finally, on the floor. She was a well-to-do girl really as she was a member of a famous, but now defunct, company that manufactured sweets. I won't mention her name, I'll just call her 'sweetie'. One thing that I remember most about her, apart from the fact that she seemed to be a bit of a nymphomaniac, was that she wore mini skirts so short that if my eyes were the same level as her skirt hem, I could see the gusset of her knickers.

She told me that she used to go to the Officers' Mess but got sick of pilots. (She thought that all of the officers in the mess were pilots.) She said that they were always bragging about flying. She related to me that she had discovered the ideal way to put a 'pilot' in his place. (She had probably bedded most of them.) It seems that one night in the mess, after she had got so fed up with this 'pilot' who had just finished lecturing the assembled group about how brilliant 'pilots' were, she said:

'That was a great story, but tell me, do you know what little owls are called?'

'Owlets,' replied the pilot.

'How about little eagles?' she asks.

'Eaglets,' answered the pilot.

'How about little pigs?' she asks.

'Easy, they are piglets,' came the smug reply.

'Right, here is a difficult one. What are little haemorrhoids called?' she asks.

When the pilot said that he did not know, she told him the answer. 'Pilots', and with that she walks out of the room.

I saw her every night after that (except for the two weekends that I drove up to Edinburgh to see Margaret) and I must admit that she taught me quite a lot about pure, hard, unadulterated and sometimes just a little bit kinky, sex.

The two weekends that I drove to Edinburgh, we just spent in the camper with the curtains closed. I suppose that we used to eat but I do not remember that at all. Some of the things that I had learned with 'sweetie', Margaret and I did in the hills surrounding Edinburgh. During those weekends we both enjoyed oral lovemaking (something that my wife would never do for me) and every other type of lovemaking that a loving couple could do for each other. I never wore any protection at all and the feeling we enjoyed was incredible.

Now was the time for me to go to Germany and for Margaret to go to Africa. My life would, from now on, never be the same again; especially my relationship with my wife.

9

RAF BRUGGEN

(German Phantom Phixers)

I climbed into my trusty, and by now, much loved VW camper (such fond memories!) and started the drive to Germany. No big deal; driving to and from Germany was an everyday occurrence for British Service-men, who would often drive home for the weekend on a moment's notice. The poor civilians used to get whole TV programmes devoted to telling them how to drive to the continent and what to do to their cars to prepare for the journey etc. What a sad lot the civvies are; and they have the nerve to say that we are 'molly-coddled' in the services!

I duly arrived at Bruggen and moved in to the mess to 'live in' for the usual minimum six weeks before my name came to the top of the housing list and I was allocated a quarter or hiring. It then took a further two weeks to actually get the quarter and 'march-in'. I was allocated a maisonette in one of the new blocks that had just been built in Elmpt; affectionately known as Legoland, as the whole of the married quarters patch looked like a big scale model of Legoland. The 'singlies' who lived in the mess blocks for all of their three years tour used to call it 'Leg-over-land', for the obvious reasons.

Anyway, after the quarter had been taken over it would then require another drive back to the UK to pick up wife and family and return them all to our new abode. However, prior to bringing our families out we had to endure the minimum eight weeks separation incarcerated in the mess. There was of course, another way of looking at it; we had eight weeks of freedom in the mess, in Germany, the land of great beer and all at duty free prices. Yahoo!

All the lads that I had done my Phantom course with had either just arrived or were going to do so within a few days of me. Some of them had been to Germany before so knew the ropes. Tasting all of the various beers that were usually 'chased' by copious amounts of duty free spirits (spirits were always served as doubles in the mess) became an interesting hazard. Technicolour yawns were usually the end result, i.e. being sick.

Many a morning I awoke to find myself in bed having no idea how I had got there. One time I remember I went into the mess for breakfast on a Sunday morning in my usual stupor, to be greeted by John with his ankle in plaster and cursing me. Apparently he had fallen into a ditch whilst drunk and on his way back to the block, and could not get out. He shouted for help in vain but then saw me. He apparently shouted 'Dave, help, get me out', at the top of his voice. I, of course, was in my auto-zombie 'go to bed' mode and did not hear a thing.

I decided to stop drinking draught Heiny after that and stuck to Amstel. It still put me into 'don't care land', but I remembered most of it the next day.

It was in the mess at Bruggen that the famous 'Drinkers Fault Finding Chart' became the accepted norm. For any of you who do not know it, it is reproduced overleaf.

I was receiving letters from Margaret and writing to her out in the jungle in that secret little way that we had worked out. I was also receiving the odd letter from my wife as well but it was Margaret that I wanted to get letters from. I definitely was in love with her and had I been a civilian we would have been in that croft in Scotland. The mess rules are quite fastidious about wives not being allowed into the mess mail-room, even though all mail for SNCOs and their families in Germany was addressed to the mess. If the husband was away anywhere and the wife went to the mess to pick up the mail, she had to ask a mess member to get the mail for her. That mess member would then give her any mail addressed to either her or to 'Mr and Mrs' but would leave any mail addressed to the husband alone.

It was a good system really, but one that used to annoy the wives no end. No doubt it saved a few marriages. No doubt it also encouraged some of the husbands (like me!) to be unfaithful if they had a mind to.

I had been posted to 17 Sqdn, which were equipped with Phantom FGR2 aircraft and I found myself as a Line Controller, a job that I absolutely loathed. I made it quite clear that I felt that I was a square peg in a round hole, especially when we had two of our aircraft crash in a two week period: they were not my fault by the way.

I eventually managed to get moved after about eight weeks on the Squadron and ended up in the BDU (Bomb Dummy Unit) bay, a new

Sympton	Fault	Action to be taken
Drinking fails to give satisfaction or taste, shirt-front wet.	Mouth not open or glass being applied to wrong part of face.	Buy another pint and practise in front of mirror. Repeat until method perfect.
Drinking fails to give satisfaction or taste, beer unusually clear or pale.	Glass empty.	Find someone who will buy you another pint.
Feet cold and wet.	Glass being held incorrectly.	Turn glass around, so that open end points to ceiling.
Feet warm and wet.	Incorrect bladder control.	Go and stand next to nearest dog. After 60 seconds complain to owner about lack of house training; demand pint as compensation.
Bar is blurred.	You are looking through the bottom of your empty glass.	Find someone to buy you a pint.
Bar is swaying.	Air turbulence is unusually high, probably due to darts match.	Insert broom handle down back of jacket.
Bar disappearing in the distance.	You are being carried out.	If you are being carried out by strangers, scream 'kidnap, help'.
You notice opposite wall is covered in ceiling tiles and has a strip light fitted.	You have fallen over backwards.	If your glass is still full, continue drinking. If your glass is empty, get someone to help you up and lash you to the bar, get the person you are next to, to buy you a pint.
Everything has gone dim, you have a mouth full of dog-ends and broken teeth.	You have fallen over forwards.	As above.
Everything has gone dark.	The pub has closed.	Curl up on floor and sleep until opening time.

bay that had been set up to look after the BDUs and their associated cradles. BDUs were nuclear weapon simulators, which were the same shape and weight as the real thing and provided the same electrical responses when fitted to the old Phantom.

Bruggen operated with two nukes, either the 550 lb or the 2200 lb, and they were both American. We rarely played with the real thing, so almost all weapon load training and loading during exercises was done with the BDU. My young SAC, my staff of one, a lad called Steve Raw, and I spent that summer spraying up the BDUs to look pristine. The paint that we used was an epoxy mix type and we did all of the spraying outside as the stuff was toxic and spread around for miles.

One weekend, when I was on 'Duty Armourer', I drove the camper into the armoury, masked it up and spray painted the top half in the good old 'nuke white'. The whole armoury ended up with every floor, door, window, item of equipment etc. having a white dusty finish glued to it. I drove the camper out and parked it round the corner and out of sight. Monday morning arrived and went; nobody noticed! Amazing!

So all of you lads who are at Bruggen today (sorry, this bit does not apply anymore as the RAF are no longer in Germany), look on top of some of the old cupboards; see all that white dust stuck to the top – that is DTD 5555 epoxy white paint used to paint nukes and VW Campers.

I should think that the only thing left of my beloved camper today is a thin shell of white paint holding the top half together.

It was on this job that my back took a pounding. We used to store all of the BDUs on type SA trollies in a wooden hut that was just past 431 MU on the ring road. I forget the hut number but on my last trip to Bruggen for a week or so it looked as if the place had been demolished. The hut had a dirt floor covered in PSP. (I never did know what this stood for. I was told once, many moons ago, that it stood for 'Pierced Steel Plate' but I have my doubts.) The Type SA trollies had BDUs on their backs complete with cradles, which made a load of 5000 lb. There were no steering dollies for the drawbar (or if there were, they were all in the USAFE SSA, we certainly didn't have any) in those days, and as the drawbar itself weighed something like 150 lbs when trying to lift it by the NATO Standard lunette eye.

Envisage the scene, me on the drawbar both lifting it up and trying to steer the trolley loaded with 5000 lbs over a PSP floor and with Steve pulling and pushing these things manually in and out of the hut. We had to get a bit of a run to actually get it out of the hut, as the track to the hut was a slope. We could only attach the prime mover, usually a Land Rover, to the trolley once it was clear of the hut.

My back was never the same after that. When I eventually left the RAF, I complained to my doctor about my back and told him what I thought had caused it, namely, the afore-mentioned job. He put me in touch with the 'War Pensions' people who sent a doctor round to examine me. The end result is that I now receive a war pension (tax-free) of circa £100 per month.

The mess life at Bruggen was fantastic. Every night was busy, mostly because of the inmates waiting their eight weeks turn to get a quarter, but any night that had a 'do' was packed to bursting. The mess at Bruggen was a good deal smaller then and quite basic. (I have been back since 'Tonka's' (Tornadoes) have been stationed there. It is very different. It is now a palace but also a mausoleum.)

Every Saturday night was a dance night. Now I, like most fellers, will only dance after a few beers to lubricate the knee joints. When I was living 'in' we were always trying to dance with anyone we fancied, but we always made sure that we had a 'duty dance'. Some fellers would dance with their wives but some would not under any circumstances. If the woman was also plain then she got very few dances at all. We, being almost temporary 'singlies', as a matter of chivalry, would always ask one of these wallflowers for a dance, and this was christened the 'duty dance'. We were only honour bound to undertake the 'duty dance' during that initial few weeks before our wives came out. I don't suppose that our motives were entirely chivalrous as, after all, she may have had a good-looking friend she could introduce us to. Anyway, the mess social life was one big party with everyone dancing with everybody else. I remember one that I used to dance with regularly. Her name was Jane Young and she never went to the mess wearing anything but a little black number. She was very nice and looked a bit like Jackie Kennedy (Onassis). I used to meet her for coffee in the 'Mally' (Malcolm Club) sometimes but somehow we never seemed to get the opportunity for more than that.

As the tour progressed we usually ended up by knowing everybody quite well. However, I actually refused the advances of one of the girls. She was part of a circle who always did everything together, you know the cliques. Her opening gambit to all of the fellas was that she had never had an orgasm in her life and when she found a man that could give her one (an orgasm that is, as a lot of the men in the mess had already 'given her one') she would have him, whether he was married or not, and make him the happiest man in the world. By the way, she was already married and with her husband at the time.

Scary!

This woman was dangerous. I might not have been very faithful to my wife but I was not going to risk breaking up my marriage for her. Even the woman I really loved had not been able to make me do that.

My marriage by now had settled into a sort of comfortable routine. My wife was a good mother and housekeeper even though our sex life had become mundane. (Is that another word for 'boring' or not?) I had my memories to dwell on. No! I was not ready to break up my marriage for anyone, and I had Jane that I could hold in my arms to imagine that she was Margaret.

What I did not realise of course was that my wife was also dancing with someone regularly. Someone who had the nickname, 'The Student Prince', and was a 'singly', not just someone waiting for his wife to join him.

We used to have exercises very regularly at Bruggen. At least every 3 or 4 weeks the old steam-hooter used to start which could be heard for miles. Three o'clock on a Sunday morning, after a night in the mess that we had only left one hour previously, did not happen all that regularly but it did sometimes. It used to go at all sorts of peculiar times, including five minutes after we had just got in to work or five minutes before we were due to go home. Mostly though it began its howl at 3 or 4 in the morning.

Our rush in to work followed a fairly set pattern with day one as a conventional war day but with the odd 'Sel-Rel' (Selective Release of a small nuclear weapon just to let them know that we would) and day two as the all-out nuclear day. When every aircraft got the order to scramble and they all took off en masse we knew that the last phase that followed pretty soon afterwards, would be that a nuke had been detonated (just an exercise remember) near us (they never seemed to get a direct hit on Bruggen, that would have spoilt the game), and the exercise would soon be over.

After 'Endex' was announced we knew that we were about halfway through the work that had to be done for that day. Everybody else of course went home for their well earned little kips, but the armourers had to find, check and put back to bed all of our kit that had been issued for the war.

Oh well, we have some crosses to bear for the privilege of being armourers.

It was during one of the exercises when, unusually, we were fitting live nukes, that my name was put, or so I was told, in front of the President of the United States.

I was the team chief of a nuke loading team, and during loading we were monitored by a USAF Tech Monitor to make sure that we did nothing wrong. There was also an armed USAF guard (real bullets) watching over us and an armed RAF guard (real bullets) watching over him; you know the score of the nausea associated with nukes, necessary though it undoubtedly is.

Anyway, we had reached the point where the Tech Monitor and I (Two-man principle, don't forget) had to go and 'take over' the weapon from the delivery crew. Part of the take over procedure was to check the weapon to make sure that everything was as it should be, especially with safety devices. Lo and behold, I spotted that the tail safe lock had been fitted the wrong way round and that it would not act as a safety device.

I pointed this out to my Tech Monitor, a USAF Captain, who at first would not believe me. He didn't believe me because he hadn't a clue what he was talking about. (It's comforting to know, or is it, bearing in mind these were live nuclear weapons, that the USAF Officers are just like our very own RAF Officers, i.e. useless.)

I finally managed to convince him that I *did* know what I was talking about and I shouted out to the rest of my crew that the load was suspended and the clock stopped. (The RAF policeman used to radio through to 'ops' when the load started and finished, as all loads had to be completed in 45 minutes.) The Captain panicked and started to transmit on his radio when he was just six inches from the live weapon. I dragged him away, by which time the USAF guard started to twitch and raise his gun, especially as the captain started running around all over the place. Twerp! And it was the Yanks who had invented the 'two man principle'.

Very soon after, everyone and his dog turned up at our revetment, which left me, and my team, time to sneak off and do the important things during our 'practice war'. We went off for one of those famous steak sarnies (sandwiches) that the 31 Sqdn. cooks used to dish up 24 hours a day during exercises.

To cut a long story short, the result of a foreign national rejecting a live American nuke on safety grounds, is a 'Broken Arrow' signal that I was told had to be passed to 'Mr President hisself' (that's what this Yank told me anyway) in person no less. Hi there, Gerald Ford, remember me?

After only a year in the BDU bay, my boss asked me if I would like to take over the missile bay. The BDUs were back to immaculate condition again and would now last for the life of the Phantoms, which were going to be replaced by pussycats (Jaguars) in about two years' time which would be fitted with British nukes.

The missiles that we had were Sparrow and Sidewinder and looked after by armourers entirely. We had our very own pet fairy in the bay, an Electronics J/T who calibrated and repaired the test sets. This fairy (by the name of Paddy) was the best electronic 'botcher' that I have ever known. He was also a con merchant who seemed to be able to get anything out of stores, so that made him a very useful guy.

The Squadrons used to have a MPC (Missile Practice Camp) every year at Valley in Anglesey and I decided that I would go with my bay lads to experience their problems and to see what it was all about. I decided that I would go, with Paddy, as the advance party, and to stay the full detachment, which was to be of four weeks duration.

As we were going to drive from Bruggen to Valley in a three ton truck, full of missiles and test equipment, Paddy decided that the standard truck seats would be too uncomfortable for my old bones, and got MT to remove the passenger seat and fit a leather one from a Rover 2000 for me. Paddy was going to be the driver.

We had a good time at Valley. One of my Sgts (Neil) decided to take his car over, so we were mobile. Now Neil was a good lad; he was also very bright. He had first joined the RAF to be Sergeant Air-crew but got thrown out, as he would not wear a jacket or tie or shoes when he was in civvies. He used to live in jeans, jumper and plimsoles and did not even possess tie, jacket or shoes. Needless to say, he never went to the mess.

For some strange reason, the local girls on Anglesey were not interested in us 'Foreign Englishmen' but the girls from Bangor University definitely were. I suppose that they thought this father figure could teach them a thing or two. I tried, I definitely tried, to teach them all that I knew; and very enjoyable it was too.

I also volunteered to go on detachment to Deccimomannu in Sardinia. This was where the 'tombs' (Phantoms) did their APC (Armament Practice Camp) to drop hundreds of practice bombs and fire thousands of rounds of ammo from the SUU 23A gun pod. It was a five-week

Jaguar 'V' and 'R' loaders with various weapons and munitions

Nuclear, biological and chemical decontamination wash at Bruggen

detachment and we were accommodated in a hotel on the beach just outside Cagliari. One of the chamber-maids kept me happy and contented, and all she wanted in return was to be fed pizzas.

Someone took a pair of binoculars, as the views from the hotel windows were stimulating. The view was of a bay with a pathway at the top of the cliff. Below the cliff were hundreds of little shallow caves and with bino's the activities of the local couples could be seen. I had never thought about it before, but a country that is almost 100% Catholic has a population that is well practised in oral sex. A little bit of voyeurism was good for a laugh.

We had used the camper to travel around and had driven it on holiday to Venice as well as various places in Germany and Holland. Unfortunately, it was now starting to show its age; the oil light started to glow at low engine speed and things like that. We had just about finished our three years at Bruggen anyway so it was decided that the camper would be sold on. I advertised it and an army chopper pilot flew down from wherever to look at it and he bought it. It was with a great deal of sadness that I watched it drive away for the last time.

My wife had decided that she wanted to return to the UK with the boys a couple of weeks before me, so that she could spend more time with her parents before our next posting. I had recently been back to the UK to buy our first house, even though my wife was never interested, saying that she would prefer to live in a council house.

Margaret had now returned to Scotland, so she had come down to 'Donny' when I was looking around houses and the opportunity was taken for some time together. Well the house was in Doncaster and the idea was that when I got back we would furnish it, my wife and the boys would live in it, and I would commute from my new unit at weekends to see them.

Once my wife had left, the neighbours revealed that she had been having an affair with The Student Prince for quite a while. Now I realised why she had readily accepted my detachments to Valley and Decci without complaint and why she did not want me to buy a house. She had wanted to go back early because 'he' had already gone back on demob. As soon as she got back 'he' had visited her at her sister's.

I had a couple of weeks to think.

The boys.

What about MY sons? No way did I relish the thought of another man being a father figure to them. Maybe I had not been an ideal husband but I thought of myself as a good father and the boys were my flesh and blood. They were ME in miniature.

I had put them into my wife, for her to feed and nourish, until they would be big enough to enter the world. So she had carried them around for nine months whilst she was pregnant, so what! My thoughts were more simplistic; a woman is like a plant pot full of compost waiting for a seed to be sown. The seed grows almost irrespective of the soil in the plant pot, the bottom line being that the children are the seed of the male, not the female plant-pot.

I returned to the UK vowing that I would try to win her back and to be a better husband.

A trophy the author made for the armourers on the squadrons to compete for after gun firing while on detachment to Cyprus

10

RAF SCAMPTON

(Sleepy Vee base)

Upon my return to the UK, I went to see my wife to see what could be sorted out.

'HE', had by now gone back down to the south coast and I think that he had wanted her to go with him. She had decided to discuss it all with me so we had a chin-wag about the boys and our marriage in general. The end result was that she agreed to give it another go. She would go with me to Scampton so that we could live in married quarters instead of me just commuting home to 'Donny' at weekends. I found some tenants for the house that I had just recently bought, and off we all went.

When I had last been on V bombers at Finningley, Scampton was considered to be the premier V unit, so I quite looked forward to going back onto the old Vee. By now, married quarters in the UK were very much easier to get, due to the fact that a greater percentage of people were buying their own houses, thus, we had already been allocated a quarter and we all arrived on camp together.

It seemed so quiet after Bruggen. Yes, the aircraft were just as noisy as the old 'tomb' but the camp itself was quiet. I put it down to the fact that this was UK and not an overseas base. All overseas bases, especially the ones in Germany, had the reputation of being more busy, and with a better social life. Work hard, play hard syndrome!

I arrived at the armoury to discover that I was to be the third 'chief' in the seat bay and man two (the jack operator) on a loading team. These jobs were exactly the same as I had done at Finningley, some 15 years ago, when I had been a Junior Technician and not the 'Chief' that I was now.

This was a body blow to my morale.

My first exercise whilst at Scampton was called at about 7 o'clock (0700 hours if you insist) in the morning; a very reasonable time I thought. Just like Bruggen and Finningley, I leapt out of bed (I was due to get out at about 0715 hours anyway, as it was not far to work from the married quarter), grabbed a biscuit for breakfast, got dressed and peddled my trusty 'treader' (push-bike cycle) to control to book-in. Pete Smith had beaten me in as he was 'The Controller' and used to get pre-warned for exercises would you believe! He told me to slow down, as nothing would happen yet. 'Ages' later, people started to amble in, including the boss, who we used to call 'Jesus Christ' 'cos he thought of himself as second only to God.

'Have you shaved this morning Chief'? he asks.

'No,' say I, 'I rushed straight in for the exercise!'

'Go home this minute and shave, and don't come in to work again without shaving.'

My gast was flabbered. This was definitely not the 'trip-wire' reaction that I had been used to! Is this man a lost soul or just a moron? (I learned later that either description would have suited him quite well!) One of the expressions that I shall never forget, which he made to me a few months later was 'Just because I did not explain it properly, is no excuse for you not to understand me.' Now I ask you, should moronic people like that run this man's Air Force? Well, I've got news for you, they already do and always have done!

Anyway, I digress. After he left to go and get a coffee and retire to his office, Pete said 'We don't get to load the first aircraft until at least 12 hours after the exercise has been called.'

What! The war would have been lost by then.

I lost all interest in work at Scampton after that and after a quick word with my wife (we used to have 'admin breaks' through-out any exercise that was called, so that everyone could go home to eat and sleep would you believe), I volunteered for the real Air Force in Germany as soon as the exercise finished.

What a farce that exercise had been. It took us two days to load not even all of the Vees. These people were living in pre-historic days and I wanted no part of it. Let them live in their steam age; there was a cold war going on in the rest of the world and I wanted to be a part of that.

Our married quarter was mediocre even though we had a nice view over open fields to the Lincolnshire Showground. There was also a path over the fields to the showground so we used to walk over and get in free whenever there was something on.

Lincoln is quite a nice city, as cities go. It was not too far to drive to, bearing in mind that almost all military airfields are out in the sticks. The Sergeants' Mess was a bit sleepy, but they did manage to have some social activities that my wife and I, along with some friends of ours, Andy and Betty, could go to.

My wife then decided that she wanted to learn to drive. I gave her a few lessons and she passed first time. (She must have had a good instructor!) We bought a little mini van banger for her, which she used to bomb around in. She also got a job in the Officers' Mess kitchen, which was quite well paid, so we were suddenly affluent. It is amazing the difference that a second income makes, and this was the first time that my wife had been able to work.

Once we had got to 'Happy Scampers' we had been able to go back to see both of our parents during odd weekends whenever we wanted to, and the time slipped by quickly to when we would be off to Germany again. I even went to see my parents to spend the odd weekend on my own. They had by now moved to Thorne.

During the first weekend, I had arranged to see Margaret so that I could tell her that I wanted to stick to my marriage. On another weekend, Margaret had asked to see me to talk things over and perhaps for us to make love for the last time. This we did, obviously, and it seemed to be about once per half hour that we were together. (Where did I find the energy?) Our lovemaking seemed so different. It was just as good, but somehow different. We parted, probably for the last time. It was a wrench but I had my two boys in mind.

Just before we were due to go to Germany, which was to be about a year later, as it happened, came the bomb-shell.

My wife had received a letter from 'HIM'. (No doubt that they had kept in contact due to the timing of this letter.) He wanted to see her to try to convince her that she should go and live with him. I assumed the worst when she said that she would go and see him to talk it over, so I started to plan my tour in Germany as a 'singlie', or as a 'second-time-singlie', as we were more correctly called.

She came back from her visit to announce that she did not know what to do, but that she had not actually seen him but just his parents. I did not know whether to believe her or not, but 'what the heck'.

Que Sera Sera. ('Whatever will be, will be', if you don't know the song.)

I left her to it. I resigned myself to her going South and me going East and that I would probably never see my children again. The courts at the time never, but never, awarded custody of the children to a serviceman. They, the wig-men who sat in courts, assumed that firstly, I was a man and therefore did not know how to look after my own children (What cheek!) and secondly, that I was a serviceman so that it would have been almost impossible for me to look after them during detachments, exercises, duties and especially during war-time.

My wife then announced that she wanted to go to Germany with me. It seemed that I had won the day.

A few days before I was due to travel out to Germany, a letter came for me at the mess. It was a hand that I recognised; Margaret.

She wrote that she had to see me soon (obviously my movement abroad was soon due) that it would be the last time as she promised that after this she would not bother me again. I drove to our allotted meeting place and I spotted her, looking as incredibly beautiful as always, walking down the road pushing a pram.

A pram. My mind raced.

She was very pleased to see me, full of joy and gushing love.

'Meet baby Martin,' she gleefully said. He looked just like Mark and Lee had done at one month of age.

Did I see Margaret just less than a year ago? I most certainly did; it was the time that our lovemaking seemed so different. We were not only making exquisite love, but also making baby Martin. She said that she had stopped taking the 'pill' when we last met and also that her husband thought that the baby was his, and that was the way she thought the situation should remain.

This all reminded me of that 1963 film called *Sailor of the King*. Except of course that I was not a Vice Admiral standing in 'Buck House' (Buckingham Palace) waiting to get a Knighthood and my, unknown to me, son was standing next to me to pick up his VC.

Anyway, I agreed! I never saw her again, although I did see Martin a few years later.

I drove out to Wildenrath, the only unit that I had volunteered for, which is why my posting took so long, in the old Austin 2200, which by now was just about on its last legs.

11

RAF WILDENRATH

(More Phighting Phantoms)

I got to Wildenrath in my old Austin 2200 which just about died as I drove through the gates, poor thing. Whilst it was a big 6-cylinder job, it did not like long distance driving at all.

Whilst at Scampton and with the extra money coming in from my wife working, we had decided that just for once, we would buy a car for space and comfort instead of putting the essential requirements like fuel economy at the top of the list. Maybe I should have considered reliability a bit more!

We had also bought a duty free FIAT 600 for my wife to use in the UK whilst she waited for me to get a quarter in Germany. It was a useful rule by dear old Customs and Excise (Did you know that the law of the land does not apply to customs men or their rule book?) that we could buy a duty free car in the UK up to six months prior to finally exporting it. Additionally, we paid no road tax during that period and had a tax-exempt disc and the usual red outline around the number plates. (I had always wondered why a very small number of cars had this red outline.)

I had not been entirely sure that my wife had been truthful, when she said that she wanted to go to Wildenrath with me; I was convinced that by the time that I was allocated a quarter she would write and say that she had changed her mind. However, she wrote loads of letters so I became less concerned about that possibility.

Wildenrath had quite a few quarters but the waiting list was a long one. It could sometimes take a year to be allocated, but there were blocks of flats that were 'hirings', dotted around the area and the waiting time for these was only about a month. I was convinced that my wife would not wait a year, so I applied for a flat and was allocated one in Erkelenz, which was about 8 miles from camp. By the time that I 'marched in' our deep-sea boxes had arrived so that our goods and chattels were already in place.

I got a lift to the boat at Zeebruge and caught a train once I was back on English terra-firma, then drove my wife, our two boys and the remains of our personal items back to Wildenrath in the tiny little FIAT; not the most comfortable of drives.

My job was running the Phantom Role Equipment Bay, SUU 23A Gun Bay and the ASF armourers.

The place was a mess, disorganised and untidy. Still, it was soon shipshape and running like clockwork. The Role Bay consisted of Inboard Pylons, Aero 27A centre line bomb rack, which still had the nuclear weapon BRSL (Bomb Release Safety Lock) installed, Aero 7A Sparrow missile launchers, Lau7A Sidewinder missile launchers, Inboard and outboard weapons pylons, Sergeant Fletcher fuel tank pylons as well as the usual array of adaptors.

The ASF (Aircraft Servicing Flight) armourers in the hangar were my 'pidgin' (responsibility) and mostly they were left alone, except for the seat 'indies' (Independent Checks) that I did.

Everybody wanted to work in the gun bay. It was the filthiest gun in christendom and the lads who maintained them were permanently black up to the elbows. However, it was a fantastic piece of kit and something that the lads could really get their teeth into. Everyone used to get great job satisfaction from working on 'the gun'. Reminds me of another film of the same name (*The Gun*) starring Frank Sinatra, Sophia Loren (what a fantastic piece of 'woman-flesh' that woman still is. Carlo Ponti was a very lucky man) and Cary Grant. Actually, the film is called *The Pride and the Passion* but I prefer to call it what C S Forester called his book from which the film was made, viz *The Gun*. That film made a big impression on me, even though I am not a Frank Sinatra fan, neither singing and definitely not when acting.

Job satisfaction was something that was sometimes difficult to obtain in our trade, as a lot of our kit was never actually used for the main purpose for which it was intended, especially the weapons like torps and missiles and the like. They were maintained then stored, maintained then stored ad infinitum.

Still, in the case of the nuke guys, that was probably a good thing.

* * *

Whilst living at Erkelenz, we soon got into the routine of travelling backwards and forwards to and from work and everyone used to share cars to make life easier. Mick Mathews and his lovely wife Joan had arrived at about the same time as us. I had known him before at various units, including BK, and so we ended up travelling to work together.

It is odd how some people seem to meet at different locations around the world. A guy who was in my entry at Halton (THE NINETY-FIRST ENTRY. Yaaa-hooo), a 'sootie' (Engine fitter, or were we Tehnicians by then?) by trade, called Bob Sayers, seemed to be at the same unit on every posting that I have ever had, usually he was either just going as I arrived or just arriving as I left. However, the great majority of the entry I never met again even after 38 years in the mob. Maybe I just didn't recognise them!

My wife had settled into the flat quite well but was getting bored and wanted a job. She was not enthusiastic about driving to camp each day on the wrong side of the road, so she kept pressing me to apply for a quarter on camp.

The rules stated that we had to stay in the flat at Erkelenz for a year before we could apply for a quarter on camp. This was the reason why the waiting list was so long, for not only were the folk just in from the UK on the list but also everyone in flats. I applied for a quarter on camp.

In our flat, our next-door-neighbours across the landing were a black couple. She was of the 'black mamma' type, quite chunky, and he was the blackest man that I have ever seen. He had a style of dancing (this is the modern shuffle type thing where people do what ever takes their fancy) where he kept his feet firmly attached to the floor but every other part of his body used to move. I tried to emulate him but me being a 'honky', I didn't have that in built body mechanism that black folk seem to be born with. I certainly envy their ability to move. They were a very nice couple, with two of the cutest kids, both little girls.

One day, we took both of our families to the zoo and the two girls and I were at the front. Liza (honest, that was her real name) was running on ahead to look at something and I thought that she was getting too far ahead so I shouted her to wait. She turned round and gave me such a disapproving look.

By now, a couple of seconds later, the rest had caught up with me and I said, 'Did you see that black look that Liza just gave me?' Then I realized what I had said and hoped that the ground would open up and swallow me. Her parents just laughed, as no doubt they were used to comments, especially from the Germans, who did not seem to approve of the black folk at all.

One night, whilst we were at a party at the next-door-neighbours and I was still trying to emulate the dancing of our host, there was a knock on the door. Our neighbour answered it and shouted that it was for me.

I was given the news that my father had died.

The RAF knew that I was an only child and they pulled out all the stops. I was driven to camp and put on a Hercules that had waited half an hour for me to turn up. On arrival at Lyneham, I was taken straight off the aircraft, wheeled through customs and into a waiting car. The RAF driver drove me home without a stop (except for fuel). Eight hours after being told in Germany that my father had died, I was home in Thorne, just outside Donny you may recall, comforting my mother. One thing that the service is good at is that sort of thing.

Even more surprising was that my wife drove back to the UK a couple of days later in her little FIAT 600 car. She had left the boys with some friends and set off. Remarkable really, considering that she had hardly driven anywhere further than about five miles at a stretch before that.

The funeral was very much like any other. I regretted that I had not spent more time with my dad while he had been alive and had never told him how much I had appreciated him and loved him. I should think that almost every child thinks the same on the death of one of their parents. I vowed to make sure that I did not make the same mistake with my mother.

A cousin of mine, who had always looked upon my mum as a favourite aunt, agreed to move in to look after her. She had wanted to move away from her parents and brothers and jumped at the chance of being my mother's live-in companion.

After a couple of weeks of compassionate leave I drove my wife and myself back to Germany.

Whilst I had been at 'Scampers' I had seen an advert in a paper for someone to sell leather and suede coats. I wrote to the company and asked them if they would send coats out to Germany via BFPO (British Forces Post Office) at duty free prices. They said they would so I started to sell coats in my spare time. Everyone posted to Germany was seemingly affluent, what with the allowances, duty free petrol, booze and coffin nails etc. Leather was very popular (even the Germans seem to live in leather coats. Remember the old war films, the German officer corps always wore leather coats in those films) and was one of the items that everyone had on their list to buy and take back to the UK.

Leather coats were selling like the proverbial hot cakes. The guy in the BFPO used to ring me up whenever parcels arrived so that I could go and get them to make room for the rest of the mail. I even had sub-agents at Bruggen, Laarbruch and Gatow who also sold a few for me.

The money that I made from the coats, enabled me to travel to the Mercedes-Benz factory at Sindelfingen and pick up my brand new Merc, all paid for by selling leather and sheepskin coats. At the same time we bought a brand new Mini for my wife.

This was the life!

Work was by now well and truly sorted and I was the senior 'Chief' in a flight that never seemed to have the Warrant Officer that we were supposed to have. We were not established for a Flight Sergeant. For fourteen weeks we hadn't got a Flight Commander either so I always seemed to be doing everybody else's job as well as my own.

Bob Beattie, who was my Sergeant, was nominally in charge of the gun bay and he spent most of his time demanding bits for the gun and building tool kits as I maintained day-to-day control of the running of the bay. The gun was a declared weapon to NATO but we didn't have enough to go round as we only had one gun per aircraft. If a gun was U/S, then an aircraft had to be taken 'Off State' as well. Needless to say, there was a lot of pressure to keep the guns 'S' (Serviceable) as every one we had counted towards our declared operational capability. I remember that we had to provide 'Ops' with our gun status every day.

One year during APC (Armament Practice Camp) in Cyprus, we had a disastrous batch of ammo. It was some cheap Indian stuff that no doubt cost a few pence per round less than our normal supplier, who I think was a British firm. On firing, the primer would blow out the back of the round and nadgered the firing pin and the breech-block.

Now, when the SUU gun had a stoppage it was usually cataclysmic. It normally chews itself to pieces over quite a number of its moving components, which is of course, most of them. Being a rotary gun of the Gatling type, it well and truly mangles itself. Bear in mind that the gun can start firing, accelerate up to a speed of 6,000 shots per minute (no, that is not a 'typo' (typing error), think about it! Think about a revolving gun that fires 100 rounds per second, each round the size of a small lemonade bottle), can slow down and stop firing in less than one second, and also bear in mind that with this gun, every single one of its 1200 rounds magazine capacity moves forwards as the gun fires, and you can imagine the momentum that builds up by the time the gun is firing at its full speed. This gun is a 'mean machine'.

Would the air-crew stop the APC to save the damage to their declared weapon? No chance! They wanted their toys to play with and did not care two hoots that the gun bay boys were working 24 hours per day and the whole of the RAF stock of spares was flying out on its way to Cyprus to enable them to continue.

We sent complete guns as spares until we had no more left at Wildenrath. By the time that the APC was finished, every gun was nadgered. As I said before, in theory this meant that the whole of Wildenrath should have been declared to NATO as 'off state' but I know for a fact that was not the case. However, there was a lot of panic to get the guns back to a 'S' (serviceable) state again. It was during this period that I experienced my one and only 'mutiny'.

We were working a standard six-day week to recover the guns. We would all work Monday to Friday as normal then half would work on Saturday and half on Sunday. This one particular weekend the Armament Flight were having a party in the section on the Saturday night. I agreed that everyone could work on the Saturday that weekend so that they could sleep off the inevitable hangover on the Sunday.

Everyone arrived to work on that Saturday at the normal time. At lunch time, I sent them off for lunch. Most went to 'The Mally' (The Malcolm Club) at noon but by 1300 hours there was no sign of them. At 1315 hours I sent Stumpy Stothard to get them back again.

They all arrived back with that tell-tale glazed look in their eyes and a strong smell of booze on their breath. They had obviously thought that it would be a good idea to get some practice in for the night's revelry. I lined them all up outside at 'attention' and asked each one individually if they had been drinking. 'No Chief,' they all mumbled.

I told them that I did not believe them and considered that they were not fit for work. I ordered each one individually by a direct order that they were to cease work, sleep off the drink, and report back for work at 1700 hours that day and that they could expect to be working the next day, Sunday, to recover the lost time.

This obviously stunned them all, as I was normally such an easy-going type. They all arrived back at the allotted hour looking very sheepish and sorry for themselves. I lined them all up outside again and 'read to them

110

the riot act'. (Not that I actually have a clue what the riot act says.) I then said that they were all to go home and get changed and bring their wives to the party, as I was not going to make the wives suffer for the stupidity of their husbands.

That party was great. All the 'bad lads' came over and bought my wife and me drinks all night long and apologised most profusely.

They also all blamed the incident on 'Stanley'. Stanley was a rebel who had been sent from MSF (Missile Servicing Flight) to me, as they could not do anything with him. He came the closest that I had ever known anyone at the time to being thrown out. Basically, the RAF wanted rid of him, but me, being a bit of a softie really, thought that he was just bored and not yet settled into the self discipline that is required of all personnel. I fought with my boss to try and keep him. I succeeded! (The last that I heard, he was a Sergeant at Coningsby.)

Where are you Stanley? Are you still in Her Majesty's employ?

One year, RAF Gatow in Berlin decided to have a big open day. Gatow was a strange place, the Station Commander's car was a big 'S' class Mercedes. This was just to look good for the benefit of the Russian guards on the other side of the wire fence who, it was hoped, would be demoralised. The unit was also a big intelligence gathering camp with a Signals Unit positively bristling with aerials. Apart from that its strategic significance was zilch.

Combat aircraft were not allowed in Berlin under the four power agreement so the open day flying would consist of 'Fat Alberts' (Hercules transports), the Gatow Chipmunks and the like. The Gatow Chipmunks were another 'Berlin' anomaly. They used to fly the border between East and West and they too had lots of funny looking aerials where aerials were not usually expected to be. They didn't fly all that often but the crew were Air Commodores and Group Captains and the like who used to cover up their rank badges with a nondescript flying suit. Also, the aircraft was crewed up and engines started 'INSIDE' the hangar with the hangar doors 'SHUT'. I assume that was the officially sanctioned way to do it and not because the 'brass' did not want to get their uniforms wet!

Once the 'crew' had the engine warmed up and all systems checked, the hangar door was opened and the aircraft would be up in the air less than 30 seconds later. It was the same in reverse, the aircraft would taxi straight into the hangar and the hangar doors closed before the engine was wound down.

Anyway, I had been asked by my boss if I would like to organise a weapons display for the forthcoming Gatow open day. I jumped at the chance as it also involved me being there for a few days.

I was given the task of organising the thing entirely for the weapons stand and arranged for a collection of guns, bombs, missiles, ejection seats and safety equipment from each of the RAFG units, plus armourers and squippers (Survival Equipment Tradesmen) to man the stand. I got 431 MU to make signs for everything in both the English and German language. I did everything from arranging transportation for us and the kit, and accommodation for all of us.

Six of us to man the stand on the Saturday and Sunday of the open day all travelled to Berlin on the 'military choo-choo'. The military train had to run down the corridor every day without fail and it was usually full of Brit military travelling on either duty or recreation. The train was a pullman type with dining cars. We were all provided with a meal, complete with wine, on the train which was served to us as the train very slowly passed through one of the East German cities, I forget which one. The whole idea was for the local East Germans to see us so that they would be dissatisfied with their lot and insurrect. It didn't work, as history proved, but at least it got us a meal and a bottle of wine for free.

One of the compartments was arranged as a spy hole with cameras and other ELINT (ELectronic INTelligence) gathering kit. Wildenrath had an aircraft on 60 Squadron that was also set up for that role and it flew down the corridor every day. No doubt the Russians were doing something similar, or maybe not as we published everything in Flight Magazine and JANE'S Books of military whatsits anyway. The Russians were renowned for doing things 'on the cheap'. The one that most people know of, is from the fact that during the 'space race', NASA, the American space agency, had spent 1 million dollars on developing a ball point pen that could be used in space where gravity did not exist. The Russians used a pencil!

When we were on the train, we had to hand in our ID cards (viz Form 1250) to the 'Train Commander'. When the train stopped at the border, he and the Warrant Officer marched up to the Russian border commander, did all the saluting stuff, and presented them to him for inspection.

Sometimes, the Russian would use delaying tactics out of cussedness, but only if the 'Train Commander' was new or had not been told of the correct procedure. The 'Warrant Officer of the Train' on our journey knew the system well and said that none of his trains had ever been delayed. As the Warrant Officer handed over the briefcase containing our ID cards, we knew that the bottle of whisky inside the case would speed up proceedings. When the case was handed back and the contents were checked to make sure that all ID's had been returned, it would of course, be minus the bottle.

Needless to say, I had arranged that we all had to be at Gatow five days beforehand to set everything up and another five days to pack it all away again. Due to our superb efficiency (!), we had the stand set up in a day and a half. The rest of the week was our own.

Now Berlin is one hell of a city! We got ourselves on one of the trips into the east of the city, that, funnily enough, were organised by the 'wives' club'. We had to be dressed in 'Best Blue', but luckily we had brought those for the open day anyway. Tramping around an 'enemy' city in our best uniforms is a strange experience. All of the East Berliners were very reluctant to either look at us or talk to us. We did the usual photo-call at Checkpoint Charlie straddling 'The Border' whilst being photographed by the East German guards. The Russkies must have had photos of almost all NATO service personnel one way or another.

We went out to the bars and strip clubs every night. The earliest that we ever got back to camp was at four in the morning. There were nights of sheer debauchery in the strip clubs. One night, which coincided with my birthday, all inhibitions went out the window, and everybody who was not rendered incapable by drink seemed to join in the resulting orgy. One Frenchman who had taken his wife and had screwed her in front of us, ended up by walking out when she decided to give several of the other lads a turn. She even tried with me but failed as I had brewer's droop; even more of a shame, she was beautiful. There were a few nights similar to that one, perhaps not quite so good, but good nonetheless. Of course, we did all the tourist things as well, it wasn't all carnal lust and satisfaction!

The Gatow 'Open Day' was actually for two days. Day One was the bigwig's private showing with Day Two as the public day. On Day One, this Russian Officer bigwig arrives with his tame 'clicker' (photographer). The bigwig tells his clicker to take 'pics' of all our weapons kit. This he promptly does by standing at one end of the display, clicking left, right and ahead; moving himself one pace sideways and taking the same three shots; and repeating the whole process until he had traversed the full length of the display. All this time this RAF clicker has his lens on my shoulder taking 'covert' (ha-ha) shots of the bigwig.

More silly games for people to play!

During the last year of my tour, my wife had got a job at the Mally, working in the paper shop. She eventually became manager of the paper shop and started standing in for the girls in the Mally bar.

I took no notice when she started to mention this poor young lad who was having problems with coping with his father's health or whatever. This poor lad had so many problems that 'one could not help but feel sorry for the poor chap, could one?'

No. one could not!

Oh dear, here we go again!

To cut a long story short she had been bonking 'Christopher Robin' and decided that she wanted him and not me. She was 15 years older than him and poor Christopher Robin had been a virgin. Poor lad! She informed me when I saw her some few months later that she had not gone with him for the sex as it was not much good for them. But hey, what did I care! My boys were now a lot older and pretty soon would be ready to 'fly the nest'. One of my ex-wife's family said years later that she now had three sons instead of two, as she used to treat her new hubby like a child. Mind, to this day they are still together so they must have something between them. Maybe he likes being a mummy's boy!

Anyway, by now we were very close to returning to the UK so we decided to split when we got back to Blighty. We drove back in our cars, she in her Mini and me in my Merc.

12

RAF CONINGSBY

(Phantom AEDIT)

During disembarkation leave I stayed with my mother in Doncaster and spent as much time with the boys as I could. My wife, although I ought to start calling her my 'ex' I suppose, and the boys had moved in to the house that I had bought whilst at Bruggen; the one that she wanted nothing to do with. It was different now of course, as the house started to have a financial value so she took more of an interest it. Strange how money changes everything! In the meantime I thought to myself 'What am I going to do at the age of forty, I'll just have to lead a lonely life'. Boo-hoo!

I started going out to a few pubs but as I was now a stranger in 'Dirty Donny' I didn't know anyone, and I'd always had difficulty in striking up a conversation with people, especially civvies.

I read in the local 'rag' of a singles club for divorced and separated people. I thought 'Oh well, I've nothing to lose.' Off I went, and to my surprise found that I quite enjoyed it. Some of the women were definitely scrubbers, not my type at all, but some of them looked really nice. It dawned on me that everyone at these clubs was the 'deserted' party in one way or the other, even if their break-up had been a mutual one. The bottom line is that we were all in the same position, all at the same level. Everyone had, more or less, been 'dumped' for another model, so all had been hurt and suffered from a dent to their ego.

However, it also made me stop and think that everyone in these clubs must have had some failing as perceived by their previous partners. That failing may have been sexual, or difference of opinion on one, or more, points. It was obviously going to be important to try to discover what that failing may have been, and whether it would bother me or not!

I started chatting with a stunning blonde called Rita. She always received backward glances from all of the men. It transpired that her husband had left her for another woman and he was living with her in a slum, whereas Rita's matrimonial home was a very nice four bed detached house in a smart part of town, in which she lived with her two youngsters. Why was her husband prepared to live in a slum with his new woman, I mused?

After we had both done the usual bit of crying on each other's shoulder about the failures of our respective previous partners (we always blame our ex partners, don't we, we never blame ourselves), I drove her home. Obviously, I tried my hand, but it transpired that she had never had sex with anyone except her husband, and that had been in bed, in the dark, on a Friday night and only the missionary position.

This was a Saturday night!

Oh dear, no wonder her husband had left her for another woman!

It was clear what I had to do. I had to teach her everything that I had learned with Kathy and Margaret. It was the only decent thing that a chap could do. I had to get her into bed, as a starter for ten, and convince her to experiment. We had talked about it, but she was reluctant, and I did not succeed with having my 'wicked-way' with her that night.

I took her out a couple of nights later and used the 'tried and tested' method of plying her with too much alcohol. That night we made love on the hearth-rug in front of the gas fire. To cap it all, it turned out that she had the very first orgasm of her life. That was the turning point, from then on we had sex in every room, in every position and at all times night and day.

In all of their married life her husband had never seen her naked and she had never seen him naked. I kept telling her that I wanted to see her naked as she had a body to be proud of. I, of course, had no problems with stripping off so she saw me naked first. I managed to remove parts of her clothing and said that her curves were a delight for me to look at. When she realised that the pleasure I got from looking at her also gave her a little tingling pleasure in the part of her anatomy that she would not talk about, it was a bonus!

It was not long before she would parade around in front of me wearing sexy clothing then inviting removal of items of said clothing, until we got to the stage where we would just have to bonk.

We did eventually get to the stage where we could just sit around together on the settee completely 'starkers' watching the TV.

There was still a big hurdle to cross though, and that was oral sex. She had confessed that her husband had tried on numerous occasions to get her to perform oral sex on him. (I bet that he was getting it from his new woman; I seem to recall that one of the nationally known soft porn stars, I forget her name, was reputed as saying in public 'Show me a woman who will not suck her husband's cock and I will show you a man who can be taken'.) Eventually I persuaded her to try and she soon became quite proficient at that, and all sexual activities, and our sex lives were very fulfilled. In fact, it soon became obvious to me that sex was the only thing that we really had in common.

One of her other failings was that she was a lousy cook. Oh yes, and another was the fact that she was very clumsy, always breaking things. I did manage to convince her that no-one is actually clumsy. Every one who confesses to this has the same trait; they don't look at what their hands (or feet) are doing. You see these clumsy people, time after time. Their hands are placing a plate on the left of them, but their eyes are looking at something completely different, to the right of them.

Result; 'Oops, it fell on the floor, clumsy me!'

After about 6 weeks or so, my disembarkation leave and annual leave ended, and I made my way to 'Big C' to earn my keep. I went into the mess as soon as I arrived on the Sunday night and 'Warned In'. I noticed that the previous line, in the 'warning in/out' book, had been filled in by Sgt Stonehouse, on the same date, and that he was just posted in like me, as opposed to 'warning in' on detachment.

I went into the ante-room looking for a post box and found just one person reading the paper. 'Could you tell me where the post box is?' I ask.

'Sorry, this is my first day here.'

'You must be Sgt Stonehouse!'

We started chatting and it transpired that John and I were in the same boat, or nearly. His wife had run off with his best friend and this was to be a fresh start for him. He had got control of his three kids as his wife did not want them. I had thought then that any woman who is prepared to run off and leave her own children was below contempt, but I don't really know why. It is not much different to a man who runs off with another woman, starts another family and never has any more to do with his first family. I had done something similar with Martin, he was my son but I made the conscious decision not to see him again. Perhaps when it comes down to it, I had no other choice.

I had been posted to Phantom AEDIT (Phantom Aircraft Engineering and Development Investigation Team) at Coningsby. The AEDITs were a Strike Command unit, lodging on whichever airfield had most of the type of aircraft that the AEDIT was responsible for. We obviously looked after 'The Tomb'.

Our little team of 'experts' (definition of 'expert' is often said to be: Ex = Past it, Spurt = a drip under pressure) existed to solve all of the problems associated with the Phantom aircraft.

The team consisted of two 'riggers', a 'sootie', a 'leccie', a 'fairy' and me. It also consisted of two Rodneys (officers), one for the 'electrickery' side and one for the 'heavy' side. The Rodney who would be writing my annual assessments was just starting to serve his 18 months notice to get out, as he had decided that he was a pacifist.

Me, an armourer being assessed by a pacifist! What chance promotion! I had a few arguments with him I can tell you.

I was travelling back to Donny at weekends to see my boys and of course, to screw Rita. However, she was beginning to pale in my eyes, as the novelty of turning her into the horny, anytime, any-place, any-position woman was wearing off.

She then also confessed that she still loved her husband. Whilst not asking the question 'why him and not me?' which was not all that good for the ego, I said that she should try to get him back, and suggested she write him a sexy letter saying that she had been reading books on sex and realised that the sex side of their marriage was staid. I drafted the letter for her, which she wrote out and posted.

She wrote to me soon afterwards saying that she and hubby were back together, hopefully for good. She thanked me profusely for the time that we had spent together and asked that I would do nothing to spoil it for them. Silly girl, I was pleased for them and she did a grand job in boosting my ego again. I had convinced myself that she had realised that she and I were not going to be 'an item' so she took the next best thing, her husband! Just in case any women are out there reading this book, thinking what an arrogant swine I am, I am not really all that vain. Honest!

John and I had sampled all the local pubs in Boston and our part of Lincolnshire but without much success at finding some crumpet. We also looked through the local rag for adverts for 'Singles' clubs but nothing was advertised. 'Where are they all?' we wondered.

John in the meantime had got his quarter and his children settled in. One of the social workers who used to visit him in his quarter, no doubt with the brief to make sure that he, as a mere male, was actually capable of looking after his children properly, suggested that he go to a 'Gingerbread' meeting in Boston.

We knew that Gingerbread was for lone parents with kids but I did not have custody of mine. It transpired that this did not matter as I was still classed as a lone parent. We went off to the Gingerbread meeting, which always used to start with everyone sitting in a circle and discussing their problems if they felt a desire to. John immediately took a shine to a very attractive, slim, blue eyed blonde who, I confess, I rather fancied myself. I looked at the remainder of the females and thought that my luck was out.

Just as I was feeling sorry for myself, the door opened and in walked a petite, slim, dark haired girl who was both gorgeous and obviously a good deal younger than me.

Oh well, nothing ventured nothing gained. I got her a chair to sit on, and I positioned it next to me, of course, and we got on pretty well. She seemed to exude happiness and joy and had a permanent smile on her lovely face. Not what you would expect from a meeting like this one. However, I found out later, that this was a facade to hide her true feelings of abject fear and nervousness. Quite a girl who can hide her fears that way!

Her name was Fay Whitfield and she asked me if I would like to go to a family dance with her the next evening. It would be a sort of social club type thing, where her father worked, and that she had arranged to go to with her parents and she would also be taking her children. On the face of it, the invitation did not sound like a bundle of laughs but as I said, this young dolly-bird really was a beauty.

The night before I had been enraptured by her lovely beaming face, but when I walked into the social club the next night and she stood up to attract my attention, my eyes went straight to her slim and shapely body and a cleavage that somehow looked incongruous. Wow! This woman, whilst being very slim, also had very large boobs that looked incredibly inviting. Her cleavage was just designed for my nose to get stuck in. Margaret had nipples that were nice to suck on, but she had boobs that were just average in size.

Fay and I got on really well and her parents were very nice too. Her kids obviously didn't know what to quite make of this new feller (she had not had any other boyfriends since separating from her husband) that their mum had invited into their life, but they were also very good. She had a boy and a very precocious little girl.

It wasn't long before I moved in. She recounted that on her wedding day she had realised at the reception that she had made a big mistake. However, she stuck it out for about eight years before finally realising that she had to get out of the marriage.

When I moved in, I was in love with her, and thought that I would spend the rest of my days with her. It did not work out that way. Yet again, the only thing that we really had in common was sex.

In that subject she taught me some things, that she said that she had always wanted to try but had never had the courage to ask, nor the partner that she had wanted to try it with. She wanted me to spank her.

That was something that I had never done, and I admit that I was reluctant, me being the perfect gent and all. However, I did spank her and it really turned her on; she became absolutely rampant. I asked her why she enjoyed being spanked so much. She explained that as she lay across my knees and lifted her skirt and dropped her knickers for me, it made her feel like she was my sex slave and that the sting of my hand on her naked bum made her pussy tingle after a couple of seconds, which resulted in her feeling so horny. She continued with that tingle in her pussy, which was then enhanced by the feeling of me as I slid inside her and of her now 'glowing' bum. She said that it made making love feel incredible.

Yes, she really enjoyed being spanked; so much so that she soon provided me with a thin willow stick, which she then begged me to use. I had learned by now that I was not to agree to her demands straight away, but was to delay as long as possible and to demand things in return that she must do for me, if I was to be good enough to spank her. This was a good game!

I had never refused any woman her sexual requests, and to cap it all she insisted that she repay me by satisfying my every whim! She wanted to be tied up, and teased, and for me to be 'The Master'. I could order her to do anything that I wanted. I used to order her to do a striptease and then get on the bed. I would tie her legs and hands to each corner of the bed and tease her for hours. I would tickle her with a feather or dangle my manhood just out of reach of her mouth. Anything that your imagination can conjure we used to do. She used to end up screaming and crying for me to bonk her, and she knew that I always would provide her with that exquisite relief from her sexual desires.

I used to take 'naughty' photographs of her with the old Polaroid camera, which she loved. She was a natural born poser. As soon as I got out the Polaroid her face would light up and she was eager to find out what I had in mind; what she needed to wear, if anything, and what I wanted her to do. We had pictures of us doing everything to each other and she loved every second of it.

Later in our relationship, she started to do something that scared the life out of me the first time it happened. At the end of her orgasm she would be out like the dead, completely motionless and not even breathing. I never quite knew what to do under these circumstances but always roused her with a shake.

I once wondered if she would come round if I did not shake her so I once timed how long she stopped breathing. She lay there without a breath for 28 seconds, by which time I started to get nervous and had to shake her quite hard to bring her back again. After that I never let her 'die' for more than about 5 seconds 'cos I was convinced that if I didn't shake her then she would never recover.

After about a year at Coningsby the Argentine nation decided that it wanted The Malvinas Islands back from us Brits who had, according to them, stolen it from them a few years earlier.

Possession being 'nine tenths' of the law and also because the islands were by now inhabited by half a dozen or so Brits who wanted an escape route from Britain, 'The Iron Lady' (Mrs Thatcher) said 'On yer bike, Galtieri.'

He, of course, was not too happy with this, and decided to take what he considered to be his anyway. The ensuing dispute in the Falkland Islands is well known and we in AEDIT were doing our bit for the war effort, everything that could be expected of us, except to be shot at of course.

I had already experienced that excitement in the desert, and I can state quite categorically that the novelty very soon wears off.

The Phantoms did not take part in the actual war, even though they were deployed to 'halfway-house' at Ascension Island to patrol the seas and protect the Task Force as far as possible, but it was well known within the service that once the war had been won then the Phantoms would be down there to keep the peace and keep Galtieri in his cage.

We all followed the war on TV at a nice safe distance, while we did all the usual contingency stuff that occurs at times like this. It is amazing where the money is found to buy all the kit that we should have had years before. I spent virtually every moment of the Falklands War writing all of the instructions for loading, fitting and installing, safety precautions etc. etc. and attending all of the meetings and trials for the fitment of AN/ALE 40 Chaff and Flare dispensers. It is amazing that we required these so urgently to fight the Argies, but obviously they were not considered important enough should we ever have gone to war with the Russkies.

One of the little tasks that we had to do was to try to find another way to fit/remove the SUU gun pod to the aircraft without using the tried and tested old faithful 'Jammer' (MJ4 Weapon loader). I looked all around 'Big C' and the only thing that appeared as if it might be suitable was the Sergeant Fletcher loading trolley when used back-to-front. I had a chat with 'Strike' who asked me to check it out. I had a quick chat with O.C. Eng. telling him that we might end up damaging one of his aeroplanes. He agreed for us to have a go, so long as no-one was around to see us and we were to inform him if we did damage a kite. We managed to get the gun pod onto the tank trolley with a gantry that we knew would be in the Falklands and then came to load the gun pod. We knew that it would be a tight fit and that we would have to have a 'run' at it. We did so, slightly scratching the underside of the 'tomb', lifted up one end of the gun into one of the hooks of the Aero 27A bomb rack and then wound the jacks (two jacks, both at one end) of the trolley down fully to lift the other lug into the second hook. Not bad really, and better than nothing. We reversed the whole process to get the gun off, showed O.C.Eng. the damage we had done (he was very relieved), and I wrote the 'war-time procedure' up and sent it off.

All the panic fitting of alien kit caused its fair share of problems and killed a few of our own lads (Harrier firing Sidewinder missiles whilst on the ground) due to the unfamiliarity of it. Needless to say that it is our boys who get the blame and not the politicians who would not release enough of the money to buy the kit earlier when it should have been first procured.

I remember one morning when the papers were full of the fact that a Vulcan Bomber had flown all the way down to the Falklands from the UK to carry out a bombing run. The next day aerial photos were released showing that the main runway had been dissected.

Funny, thinks I, a one thousand pound bomb should make a bigger mess than that, it all looks very neat and tidy. It *was* too neat and tidy, in fact the whole picture was of little circular mounds of earth to look like bomb craters. The Argies were not very good at trying to hoodwink us and it certainly fooled no-one, especially the boys in the RIC (Reconnaissance Intelligence Centre).

A couple of days later another Vulcan made the same journey to carry out the same bombing run but this time the bombs actually exploded as advertised.

'Rumour Control' had it that the first aircraft flew all that way down there and that the 'fly-boy' (aircrew) FORGOT to set the fuze control in the aircraft to make the bombs go 'Bang'. Funny that when officers make mistakes, no-one seems to hear about them as it is hushed up as much as possible!

I think that the Vulcan guys were less prepared for combat than the 'Tombs'. The big VEE bomber had never fired a shot in anger and here it was, within a month or so of going to the big airfield in the sky (scrap heap), and the Vulcan 'fly-boys' were having a wind down, when it was called upon to do its bit.

The conventional bomb carriers had already been sold off to the local 'scrappie', and the RAF was a bit red-faced when they had to go into Lincoln to buy them back again. Sidewinder Missile Launchers were bolted to the wing with angle iron and big nuts and bolts and various other bits of kit were hastily fitted (known in the trade as being 'nailed on') for that one bombing run.

Soon after The Falklands 'do' my mother died. I had got the usual compassionate leave sorted out when the doctor sent a message saying how ill she was. When I had been home for about eight days, the doctor asked me when my compassionate leave was due to end. I told him when I was due back and he then said that he thought that my mum would die that night. I answered something along the lines that it would be a release for her from the pain. (She had cancer.) He gave her some pills that evening 'to help her sleep' and she died in the night.

I am grateful to that doctor!

Being an only child, everything was up to me. My cousin Jan was helpful but in the main I had to make all the arrangements myself. At the funeral, I regretted that I had not really kept my promise to look after her properly, but it was too late now. On her last day I had managed to thank her for everything that she had done for me, which I think she heard and understood.

I told Jan that she could stay in the bungalow rent and rate free until she found somewhere else. I also said that if she wanted anything of my mother's she could have it. I then went back to work and living with Fay. A couple of weeks later, I got a solicitor's letter stating that Jan was going to apply to the court to claim that she was treated as a daughter of the family.

What!

I contacted a solicitor to find out what this was all about and it transpired that she was going to claim half of the estate. This caused me to make a few abrupt phone calls to her, and she dropped her claim.

I used to ring her about once a week to see how she was getting on with finding somewhere else to live. One weekend there was no answer. I tried again the next weekend and still no answer. The following weekend I went to Retford to find that she had moved out and had taken almost all of the contents of the house with her. What a mess she left that house in. Oh well, time to sell my mother's house.

I had been living with Fay for about two years, and by this time the sex slave bit was wearing a bit thin. We had done everything that could possibly be done by two consenting adults of different sex but there was something missing. I just wasn't content in other ways. I decided that I was going to buy my own house and do my own thing.

I bought a bungalow in New York. Not New York of New York fame but the little sleepy hamlet of New York, Lincolnshire. I enjoyed having my own space and Fay still confessed her love for me. Obviously, I was visiting her for weekends and nights and our sex life was still as good. In fact she kept giving me dates to visit that were at the high-risk points of her menstrual cycle, as she wanted to have my baby. At my age I was not too keen on starting another family, but we had been together for a couple of years now and whilst I had always ridden 'bare back' she had not conceived.

The main advantage to having my own house was that I would have plenty of space for my boys to visit. They each had their own room which they could do what they liked in, and I enjoyed looking after them, three fellers together and all that male bonding thing.

One of the female neighbours started visiting regularly for chats and cups of tea and it was obvious that she was making herself available. However, I did not fancy her and my assumption was right, as it transpired that she had wanted an escape route from her husband, and thought that I might be a suitable candidate. After I had made it clear that this was not going to be the case, she asked if she could bring one of her colleagues from school (she was a schoolteacher) to see the house.

Strange, thinks I, but she half convinced me that she had told her friends about this guy (me) who had moved in on his own and 'kept the house better than any woman'. A suitable evening was arranged and the neighbour trooped in with Jennie.

'Like a drink?' I enquire. 'Here, let me introduce you to Glayva.'

After opening the second bottle, the neighbour says to Jennie 'I think I'll go back home to bed, are you coming or are you staying here?'

'I'll stay here' says Jennie. And so she did, for the rest of the weekend. It seemed that I didn't have a lot of say in the matter. Still, who am I to complain if a woman wants to sleep with me! All I can say is 'Tally ho, away we go.'

Now Jennie had a flat in Skegness. This meant that I used to have weekend breaks in Skeggy with Jennie looking after my every need, and weekend breaks in Boston with Fay looking after my every need, and some weekends at home with the boys (they didn't need much looking after).

My daily routine during the week when I was at work, started with me pedalling off to camp, and eating a full and hearty breakfast of grapefruit, cereal, full fry-up, coffee and toast etc. in the mess before cycling to work. The mess at Coningsby was superb, with great food. We used to choose our evening meal at breakfast time from a menu of about 12 choices, including 'Roast of the Day'. Lunch would be a cup of tea from our section tea swindle and a few biscuits that I kept in my desk drawer. The evening meal consisted of the whole nine yards of soup, full roast, sweet and then coffee and biscuits in the ante-room, whilst I read the papers and/or watched the TV to let my meal digest. After that I pedalled home.

This was the life. No cooking or washing up to do except when my boys came to stay, and sex on tap. I thought that I could easily hack this lifestyle for the rest of my service career but I knew that the Air Force would soon think of something to spoil it all.

Work was interesting and sometimes quite challenging. Job satisfaction is an important factor in life. One of the advantages of service life is that if you don't like your job, you can soon get posted and move on to another one. Everyone in AEDIT used to do a lot of travelling around the other Phantom Units as well as HQSTC (Head Quarters Strike and

Training Command) as it was called then, and to 'British Waste of Space' (as British Aerospace is affectionately (?) known throughout the service) at Brough and Holme-on-Spalding-Moor (HOSM, phonetically called hozz-em). Moreover, we all got to Germany at least once per year. It was a good way to keep our 'Duty Free Stock' topped up.

The lads in AEDIT were a good bunch and saved the Air Force a lot of money. We produced the goods far cheaper than the company. I remember one incident where John the rigger had to sort out the fitting of a new piece of engine monitoring kit called a Low Cycle Fatigue Counter (or LCFC as it would normally have been abbreviated to but in this case used to be called the Lincoln City Football Club). BAe had said that it could be fitted behind panel whatever. John went to have a look to find a big black electrickery type box already there. BAe insisted that there was nothing behind this panel. John and a guy from Command went to HOSM to prove to them that they were wrong. Sure enough, upon opening the appointed panel a big black box stared them all in the face.

The RAF actually got a bill from BAe for the time that had been spent by the company in being proved wrong. Strange people; even stranger was that the bill was actually paid. That's what the PDS (Post Design Service) contract stated; time spent discussing problems were to be paid for!

Bill Barrie and I went off to visit STCAAME (STC as before, Air to Air Missile Establishment) as we had produced an algorithm to use during investigation into Missile misfires/hangfires and the like and we wanted to run it through ('verify', in correct terminology) with them. We stayed for about a week or so and had driven there by the quick motorway route. Bill and I used to get on very well and he once said that he considered me to be a good armourer, 'cos I was an old armourer and still had all my fingers and toes. (I suppose that was a compliment?)

This was not always the case with armourers, especially in the bad old days of detonators when quite a few armourers lost fingers. Additionally, in the early days of Mr Martin and Mr Baker's 'bang' seats it was reputed that they killed and injured more armourers than they saved air-crew. Thankfully, very few armourers are now injured by ejection seats and thousands of air-crew have been saved.

On our way back to Big C we decided to come back 'the pretty way' (as you do)! The pretty way of course was over Mount Snowdon.

It was the middle of summer and we were both very hot in our MT (Mechanical Transport) Section 'trusty steed' (Mini-van). We had passed a few mountain streams when we looked at each other and obviously had the same thought. I stopped the van at the next stream, where we both took off our shoes and socks, rolled up our trousers to our knees and went for a paddle in the ice cold water.

There we were, both fully grown Chief Technicians in uniform paddling like kids.

One of my trips was to Leuchars and I took the opportunity to see if I would be able to see Baby Martin. It was a fine day and I stood outside the house and watched a group of boys playing in the front garden. One of them was the right age and looked just like Mark and Lee had looked at that age. I watched for a few minutes but before any passers-by had time to think that I was a paedophile or something I left, not even speaking to him. Difficult!

Bill Barrie was a fairy (Radar) and mad keen on DIY. He came in to work one day and said 'That's it, Dave, I've finished the house, now I can sit back and enjoy it.'

A week later he came in to announce that he was selling it. He had realised that since he had nothing to do he was bored so decided to sell up and buy another wreck and start all over again. He asked my advice on whether to try to sell privately or put it into the hands of an estate agent. I said 'Try privately at first and then if you have no joy use an estate agent.'

He came in to work a couple of days later saying he had just put it straight to an agent.

The next morning, very annoyed, he said 'I've sold the house.'

'But why are you so annoyed?' I ask.

'Because the guy that bought it lives in my street and used to walk past my house every morning on his way to work. He always used to say to himself that if ever my house came on the market he would buy it. All I had to do was to put a sign in the window like you said and it would have sold. Now I have to pay the estate agent for nothing.'

Poor old Bill, a Scotsman, having to pay out good money to someone for doing nothing more than sticking a sign in the garden.

By now those horrible Air Defence Tornado things were being built and the first unit to get them would be Coningsby. All of the Phantoms would eventually be replaced but it was announced that the AEDIT would very soon move to Wattisham. I knew that the Air Force would spoil my life of leisure. I didn't fancy Wattisham and I would not have been able to commute daily, as me being a 'singlie' meant that they would not pay my travel expenses. The married men who commuted daily were paid their travel. Even though the Air Force preferred singlies as they were less trouble they victimised us by not treating us as well as the scaley's.

Time to move on, I thinks! Where do they need plumbers? Someone mentioned Belize, a six-month tour then back to an area of choice in the UK. Sounds good, maybe I can get back to Coningsby and my house. Apart from anything else I did not want to sell the Merc, and I could lay it up in my garage for the six month period.

The author dressed as a Mexican peasant in Belize for a 'Mexican Night' in the Sergeants' Mess

13

RAF BELIZE

(The best kept secret in the Air Force)

Our VC10 aircraft flew out of Brize Norton on a cold and damp 3rd of January. The first leg of the flight was over the Atlantic to Gander in Newfoundland. This is the shortest distance from UK to stateside, which the aircraft had to take as the poor old Vicky10 could not carry enough fuel to get any further. Being an old aircraft, it was not very economical in the fuel stakes and any headwind caused problems.

After an hour or so at Gander, with a temperature of minus 12 degrees, we took off to our next refuelling stop at Washington where the temperature was minus 1 degree. Another wait of about 4 hours and then the final hop down the eastern seaboard over Mexico to Belize. The door was opened at our tropical paradise and an invisible force hit us like a hammer blow. The temperature was 35 degrees Centigrade.

Belize was such a small unit and an 'operational theatre' to boot, with everyone being such a vital cog in the wheel, that no-one would be allowed to fly out on posting back to the UK unless their replacement had actually set foot on Belizean soil.

Needless to say, everyone due posting back to the UK had a great deal of interest in the manifest of the incoming aircraft that would be bringing their replacement out. Everyone would find out his name, and then find someone who knew what they looked like. Once the aircraft had landed many faces anxiously looked for that one man who was to be the replacement. Once seen, his predecessor would seek him out and show him where he was to live for the next six months. As it was 'hot' beds in Belize then the successor used to occupy the bed of the predecessor.

One of the replacement lads who was flying out with me got something stuck in his throat whilst he was in the departure lounge at Brize Norton and was rushed off to hospital. His predecessor was not a happy hector when he was told that he had to stay in Belize for at least another month until another replacement could be sent out. Poor lad, there he was, fully cleared from the unit, his jungle uniform handed back in, his belongings packed, money changed back into Sterling and to cap it all, he had passed his girlfriend over to one of his mates. Shame!

I don't suppose that his wife in the UK was all that pleased either.

I had about half an hour with my predecessor ('Swish' Cane) and that was it, he boarded the aircraft and flew out. My deputy, a Sergeant from the bomb dump called Ross, said that he would explain everything to me in the bar. My first taste of Belizean liquid was just a coke, but it was ice cold.

One of the first things that we had to do was to attend the 'New Arrivals' course. This is standard procedure on many camps, especially overseas.

This was the usual stuff of zeroing your personal weapon (yes, every man had his personal weapon allocated to him which he was to be issued with as soon as any hostilities occurred) and being briefed on why we were there and all the nasty diseases that could be obtained so easily from the local lassies. We were informed that the only way to ensure that these nasty diseases were not obtained, was to decline their kind invitations to bonk them. However, if we did insist on doing so and thereby not taking the good doctor's advice, then the 'Rose Garden' was out of bounds again, but a list of a few other bars that had been cleared was available for all to view at the guardroom.

The camp 'Dick Doctor' (some grunt sergeant) used to check out all the girls to ensure that they were clean and to give them their '6 monthly' certificate of freedom from diseases. What a fantastic job! I wonder how the girls used to pay him to ensure that they got a clean bill of health?

My first morning at work was a tour of my empire.

As a Chief Technician I was the senior armourer on the unit, so anything armament was my pigeon.

The unit had four Harrier GR3s and four Puma choppers. The Harriers used to operate from two 'hides', one either side of the runway, and the Puma's from the big hangar in Williamson site, which also included other buildings for main stores, POL, MT, GSE and workshops as well as the Armament Role Bay which had a Corporal and a Junior Technician armourer to look after second line maintenance.

My office was a trailer hut in Williamson site, complete with desk and all the armament documents and AP's (Air Publications). I took it upon myself to keep the APs amended. On the other side of the runway, past the two hides and around the 'Yellow Brick Road' was APC (Air Port Camp). About four miles away was the bomb dump (or Explosive Storage Area as it was officially termed by we RAF types, but an ESH as it was called by the Army lads. No, I never did find out what it stood for.). The 'dump' had my deputy, who was the aforementioned Sgt, a Corporal, two SAC armourers and a solitary Corporal 'blanket-stacker' (Store-man). I was also responsible for the armament aspects of the Sergeant and Junior Technician in each of the hides, but they were not 'mine' in any other sense.

The APC (Air Port Camp) was the main domain of the 'grunts' and was also the domestic area for everyone except the Harrier hide guys, who lived, worked and entertained in their respective hide.

The military set-up in Belize was that it was run by the grunts, whose boss was a Brigadier. Our boss was a mere Wing Commander and entitled 'The Air Commander'.

The grunts and we blue jobs never have got on. Bearing in mind that one of the main aims of the military is to defend democracy, it is a shame that the grunts don't even know the meaning of the word. Viz: an RAF Sergeants' Mess is run on democratic lines but a grunt Sergeants' Mess is run by the whim of the GSM (Garrison Sergeant Major). The mess committee nod their heads in agreement to everything that the GSM utters. The RAF refused to have their man on that committee.

I was lucky in that for most of my tour, the duty regiment (the grunts also did six month tours) was The Gurkhas who, as far as I am concerned, and to most people who have come across them, are, to a man, 'Little Brown Gentlemen'. Unfortunately, during my last two months they were replaced by The Paras, who are exactly the opposite.

Apart from the personnel to provide kit for the aeroplanes ('Jets', as the young steely eyed fly-boy killers seem to call them these days), I had a lone Junior Technician in 'Small-arms'. Now the RAF armoury was a 'Cage' within the grunts' armoury. All the regiments who had folk in Belize had their own cage so the RCT (Royal Corps of Transport), REME (Royal Electrical and Mechanical Engineers), RAOC (Royal Army Ordnance Corps, the people that we dealt with most, who we called the 'Rag And Oil Company'), 'F' Troop ('F' Troop was the name given to the little SAS unit that provided jungle training. They were named after the TV series of the same name, if any of you can remember that far back), etc. as well as the RAF and the duty regiment who each had all of their small arms in their own cage in the one armoury building.

The only cage that was permanently manned was ours.

The grunts used to look after their guns better than the average RAF guy so we needed someone to maintain the weapons and do issues etc. for the LAG's (Live Armed Guards). One of my first jobs was to check on the security of my inventory and I started with small arms. I was chatting to the Junior Technician and said that the next day I would go with him to check out the keys procedure. He said that it would surprise me.

We went to the guard-room and he asked the duty grunt for the keys to the armoury main building. He was given the bunch of keys but not asked to sign for them or show any identification! We then went to the QM (Quartermaster's) store, where the RAF cage keys were kept for some reason, and knocked on the steel door.

'What do you want?' came a voice from behind the steel.

'The RAF cage keys,' my man shouted back.

'I'll throw them out the window,' came the steel response. The window was above the steel door and out came the bunch of keys.

Ha-Ha, very funny, thinks I. This is some sort of joke, they are trying to wind me up! No identification asked for, nothing signed for and keys given to someone not even seen.

During that day I briefed a RAF lad, a non armourer, who happened to be black (just like the locals of course), who had just arrived in Belize like me, and told him to follow the same procedure wearing civilian clothes and not to offer to show any identification or sign anything unless asked. I followed at a discrete distance. Without any problem he was given both sets of keys in the same manner, and without any signature!

Within minutes I was relating this procedure to O.C.Eng., who was a Sqdn Ldr, who went ashen when I told him that from this point I relinquished all responsibility for the weapons held on my inventory, until this ludicrous system was sorted. He said that the next day he would like to see if his son could get the keys. Now his son was 14 years old and looked it but he also got the keys without any problem or signature. New rules were hastily introduced to the grunts, who always seem to give the impression of being very lackadaisical.

Grunts, what are they?

Good job we have an Air Force.

There were very few accompanied posts in Belize. The RAF only had about 15 accompanied and the rest, about a couple of hundred or so, were unaccompanied. This meant that there were lots of married men who were spending six months away from wifey and it gave them a chance to let their hair down.

Now most fellas will let their hair down with booze, or women, or good clean living type things like camping and sightseeing. In Belize it was easy to achieve all of these things. For the single men there were no food or accommodation charges to be taken from their pay, as Belize was considered to be an operational theatre, and in addition, pay was further enhanced by a generous LOA (Local Overseas Allowance). The married unaccompanied men were paid SEPAL (SEPeration ALowance) as well as the LOA. Consequently, everyone had lots of money to spend in the local economy and it was well known that British Forces in Belize contributed 9% of the countries GDP (Gross Domestic Product).

The first option for letting hair down was the booze. This was all duty free of course and most people drank the local rum called 'Tropical Charcoal' which was cheaper to buy than water. There was also the local beer, which was brewed just outside of the APC gate. This was called Belikin and supposed to be a lager. It should have been OK as the Brewmeister was a genuine German. However, it was the proverbial gnats-piss and had as much taste and kick as a plastic dildo. (Not that I have ever tasted a plastic dildo of course!) The only advantage was that it was served ice cold, as all drinks were in Belize. The new arrivals usually start out by drinking more than the three or four that the old-timers used as starters but soon discovered why it had the nickname 'belly-ache'. Some people tried the Yankee beers but these were just as bad as belly-ache.

Nights in the mess would consist of a few pints of ice-cold belly-ache, followed for the rest of the drinking session with rum. By the time that the 'rum run' started, all the RAF guys who would be in the mess that night would be seated at 'The RAF Table' under the atap in the mess. An atap was a grass-roofed building that had no walls at all, just wooden poles to keep the roof up. Ataps were all over the place in Belize, ranging in all sorts of sizes.

Anyway, back to the booze.

The first bottle of Charcoal with its mixers would be bought. Most things can be mixed with Charcoal and my preference was grapefruit juice. Others liked mango juice or peach (this was a favourite of the poofter chopper air-crew for some reason) or coke or lemon or whatever. One guy I knew even tried mixing Charcoal with beer, but he was really ill the next day and swore never to try it again.

Needless to say, everyone was always 'calling for Hughie' and hangovers were the order of the day for the next morning.

The next of the bad habits of hair-letting, were the women. The Belizean philosophy on sex was completely different to ours. If you took a girl home then you walked straight past her parents and went to bed, that was the norm and this on the very first meeting. Sex to them has the same status as shaking hands does in this country. Viz: you do it with almost everyone that you know!

Almost all girls had at least one baby by the time that they were 16 and the generally held view was that the father of that baby was likely to be the girl's uncle, cousin, brother, father, some other relative or someone known to the family; in that order!

They have a rather strange custom in Belize. When the baby is born the afterbirth is all scooped up and put in a pan and slowly boiled. When cooked, the mother of the baby eats the solid part of the afterbirth, and the father of the baby drinks the remaining liquid. In fact the liquid has a local name, which is 'Gumagarugu water'. They have even written a calypso song about it.

It sounds like cannibalism to me but there we go.

The Belizean women were keen to get a 'rich' (which we were, compared to the local fellers who were mostly unemployed) white boyfriend whether he was married or not.

There used to be a dance in the mess every Saturday night and the place used to be alive with women. They preferred the RAF guys as they said that we used to treat them properly. (Whatever that means!) As a last resort they would go with a grunt, but only on the recommendation of another woman who had 'sampled' him previously (the jungle drums in Belize spoke of good white men and bad white men).

They were particularly eager to find a single Brit to latch on to, in the hope of marriage, thus enabling her to get into Britain. Obviously, I was going to have to be careful. A young lad in the armoury had just applied for permission to marry one of them. (While based overseas, permission had to be sought from the Commanding Officer to marry a foreign national.) It was the general policy of the service to discourage marriages in Belize and it was the sneck's (SNCOs) job to try to talk the young bucks out of it. However, permission was rarely refused, as all that the lad had to do was to take her back to UK upon his return, where he could marry her without permission. In any case, the girl was usually pregnant, presumably the lad being the father and not someone else. I got them both in for an interview (she brought her child from some previous relationship with her) and she did seem to be a very nice girl as well as being a cracker, a real 'belter'. He was very enthusiastic, and said that he would take her back to the UK to marry, if permission was not granted. I informed the boss that permission may as well be granted and he signed the appropriate paperwork.

When the happy couple went back to the UK it was to a posting to Leuchars, just outside Edinburgh, and in February. Poor girl, I wonder how long she was happy for!

Some of the lads took advantage of the 'having to apply to get married' rule, by promising every girl they met that they would marry them, only to say later that they could not get permission. What swines some men are! However, some of the girls got their own back by passing on all sorts of venereal diseases to the lads.

Every Tuesday was the dick doctor run. All the lads who had the proverbial 'itch', used to climb onto the three tonner that was laid on to take them to the quack for their check-up. It was almost a sport seeing who was on the lorry for that week!

They would be informed of the results a week after the following Thursday. Thursdays was also the dick doctor run, but only for the guys to obtain their results. The days leading up to their appointed Thursday were usually spent quietly.

When results were known, there were sometimes glum days.

I remember three lads who had been to one of the cayes for a weekend and had met an American girl. All three had taken their turn with this girl and all three were on the three tonner on the Tuesday. Results day showed that one had thrush, one had gonorrhoea but the third had 'Big H', namely Herpes, which still has no known cure. To make matters worse, the third one was the only married one, and he would have had to tell his wife that he had Herpes for life.

Imagine the scene upon his return.

'Hello Dear, what have you brought me back from Belize?' she asks . . .

One of the lads who worked for me in the Role Bay in Williamson was a young singlie called Steve who had volunteered for a year's tour. The advantage of a year's tour was that you could take the whole of a year's leave within that year. If only on a six month tour then the only leave that could be taken was two weeks R&R (Rest and Recuperation). This was another grunt invention, a good one this time, where we had the two weeks leave but it was not taken out of our annual entitlement.

Steve was a travelling man who, strangely enough for an armourer, had no interest in booze or birds. He used his leave to travel all over North, South and Central America. His last trip was just after I had arrived, and it consisted of flying to Miami, bussing on the old Greyhound to Los Angeles, on the other side of the country, crossing the border into Mexico on the Western seaboard, and then bussing all the way back to Belize on the Eastern seaboard, the full width of Mexico. Now most people don't realise just how big Mexico is. Next time you are near a map of the world, just have a look. It is a BIG place! It did go to show though that a good clean living life could be had.

The reason that the military was in Belize was to counter the threat from Guatemala. Now the 'Gwats' had decided that Belize should be part of Guatemala, primarily because they wanted access to the eastern seaboard of Central America. At the border between the two countries on the only 'official' crossing point, the Belizean's had erected a big map of 'Free Belize' facing the Guatemalans, who in turn had erected one that showed Guatemala and included the area of Belize as just being a county of Guatemala.

A bit like Saddam Hussein did with Kuwait. All very silly!

Since Belize was part of the British Empire we had to protect them. Most people will remember Belize from their school days as being British Honduras, but they changed name on independence.

Accommodation was so tight, due to the build up of personnel, that all single rooms were doubled up. I shared a room with Big Ron who was 53 years of age and a Ground Equipment man by trade. He was out every night with his girlfriend (she was about forty) and he was as happy as Larry. He used to say that whilst he would never leave his wife, his black girlfriend was a billion times better in bed and also used to treat him like a king. He said that this was his one and only fling in all of his married life and he could now go back to his wife and spend the rest of his life in retirement with her and be content with his memories.

'Good on yer, Ron!'

When I did my Pre-Belize course at Wittering, someone said that if I could get a bike out to Belize, I would find it very useful. I took his advice and got hold of a cheap little 'shopper' type bike, took it to bits and packed it in a box to send out by sea. I re-assembled it as soon as I got out to Belize, and there I was, mobile!

I could always get hold of a land-rover or something to patrol my empire, but cycling was good exercise, especially on Belizean roads. I use the term 'roads' very loosely! Even the best of the roads were on a par with the very worst in the UK, and that is saying something. Nevertheless, I used to bike around my empire performing my management function, which mostly consisted of chatting to all and sundry.

One day I went to see Tony in whichever hide he was in; I think it was 'Foxy Golf', or maybe 'Charlie Delta', I never could remember which was which! This particular hide was the one on the 'Williamson' side of the runway, which was approached down a grotty old jungle track full of pot-holes.

Just before the hide was the Belizean airport fire crew. Tony once told me about a Cessna aircraft that had run out of fuel whilst on its way to the airfield, and just managed to crash land onto the runway. The RAF fire tenders were there first, of course, and as they were cutting the two survivors out of the wreckage, the Belizean fire chief turns up and says to the survivors 'good job there is no fire man, you are just lucky there was no fuel on board.'

He never did realise how ludicrous that statement was. Anyway, I digress.

For some reason I was in a hurry to see Tony and had built up a fair speed on my bike by the time I got off the road and onto the track. There I was hurtling down this track at a fair rate of knots, swerving around the pot-holes, when all of a sudden I noticed that straight in front of me was this rather large snake. In fact it was about eight feet long.

It was at this point that time stood still.

I thought about a similar sized snake that I had seen a few days earlier, that a Land-Rover had run over, and the snake had turned its head around and tried to bite the Rover, which was left with about four sets of twin venom stains down its side. I thought of all the nasty types of snakes that lived in the jungle, like the Feu de Lance, which was reputed to have a venom that could kill in seconds and for which there was no antidote.

I thought about going into the pot-holes to try to miss it, but if I did I would most certainly come off, due to the small wheels of the 'shopper', and no doubt crash onto the snake anyway. After a nano second had elapsed since I had realised this thing was straight in front of me, I had considered all of the possibilities and come to the conclusion that I was going to go over it and lift my legs as high as possible out of the way.

Time started again, and I was amazed to discover how high I could get my legs, and even more surprised to discover that I had not been bitten.

After Tony plied me with tea to calm my nerves, I was recounting my tale of near death to a group of about six of us, all stood in a circle, when a rat ran from the jungle through the middle of us, hotly pursued by an 8 foot long snake, also straight through the middle of us. They both disappeared under the dining portacabin.

We all looked at each other in amazement, then promptly fell about laughing. All the usual comments followed about the snake not being able to eat me, so had gone after some other, smaller rat instead. You know the thing!

One of the strange quirks about service personnel is that they greet their friends with obscenities. If a guy meets another and says something like 'What are you doing here you posby old ratbag,' and the response is something like 'You can talk you fat, ugly, useless excuse for an armourer,' then you can rest assured that they are good friends.

There's lots of wild animal life in Belize, most of it living within six inches of where we lived and in the case of the bugs, actually lived with us. There was a local who was employed to de-bug all of the buildings every day. He had a machine that was nicknamed 'swingfog' that used to run on kerosine and DDT. (Still using that horrible stuff) It quite literally put out a fog of this lethal combination to kill all the bugs. Needless to say, whenever the swingfog man was around we disappeared. I suppose it worked for a short time but the wee beasties soon came back again.

Some of the animal life was harmless but most of it seemed to have the reputation that it either wanted to eat you or just kill you anyway out of spite. At the time of year when the land-crabs were on the march, they were more of a nuisance than anything, but they could give a nasty nip. A night-time trip to the toilet block wearing the usual flip-flops and towel could be a hazard, as you had to kick them out of the way. No simple feat when you are half asleep and also half cut from the previous night in the mess.

Just the act of going to the toilet involved a strict BF ('Before Flight' maintenance). This procedure consisted of inspecting all around the pan for snakes, lizards, landcrabs, scorpions, tarantulas and the like. I remember once sitting in a small atap with one of the local girls late one night, when I felt something fall from the grass roof onto my shoulder.

While the senses in my eye were still sending the message of what they had seen to my brain, I became aware of another movement, which was the girl's hand as she swept the black scorpion, that was only half an inch from my face, off my shoulder. I gave her a bottle of rum and a good bonking as thanks.

Some of the wildlife was valuable. A butterfly called 'The Belizean Blue' was worth about US$300. People were always on the lookout for one. One flew into the hangar in Williamson once and all the chopper people went frantic trying to catch it. Needless to say, it got away. I don't recall ever having seen one!

Each of the Sections around the unit had their own tame section pet. Most of course were not tame at all. MT control had a tarantula, which they kept in a cage. The macho members of the unit would arrange to have a photograph of it sitting on their bare arm. Yeugh, I hate spiders. I was content to have my picture taken with a six foot Boa Constrictor around my neck. At least as it tightened its grip, it could be pulled off by the rest of the lads. It is times like that you find out who your friends are!

Over in the dump we had Ollie. He was an alligator. (Or are they crocodiles in Central America? Ollie the crocodile wouldn't have had the same 'ring' as Ollie the Alligator.) He was about seven feet long and used to live in his larder. There was a stream, which ran through the dump, and it was dug out in the middle to provide an emergency supply of water in case of fire. The resulting lake filled with flowing water and became a bit of a breeding ground for the fish. Ollie used to spend most of his time on the bank of the lake but every now and then he would leap into his larder for a meal. What an easy life he had; except for one minor little niggle.

Our 'little brown gentlemen' have a basic philosophy in life when it comes to food and that is 'if it lives, then kill it and eat it'. Being enterprising folk they were always on the lookout for things to eat. This meant that when they were guarding the bomb dump they were always trying to catch Ollie to eat him. No matter how many times they were told to leave Ollie alone, he eventually went missing. No matter really, for shortly afterwards, another slightly smaller 'Ollie Two' appeared and encamped on 'Ollie One's' patch. The Gurkha's denied most emphatically that they had eaten him, but we know that they had.

Ollie Two became relatively tame. He had a passion for compo cheese (we had to get rid of the stuff somewhere, it was revolting). The Corporal, Brian, had got to the stage where he could feed Ollie from a tablespoon held on an outstretched arm but nobody else could get within 20 feet of him before he did that frantic thrash of the body before leaping into the water (or leaping at you, as some people used to tell the tale).

The Gurkha's eating habits were once useful to us. A small group had been on patrol in the jungle and were on their penultimate day before being picked up by chopper. One of them spotted a wild boar (a peccary, for the purists) and promptly shot it with his trusty SLR (Self Loading Rifle).

What he did not realise at the time was that wild boar tend to live in herds or colonies or whatever the collective noun is for these things. The rest of the boar 'group' did not take too kindly to one of their colleagues being shot by this invading army, so promptly declared war on the whole Gurkha nation.

What had started as a clinical strike by the Gurkha, resulted in a mass retaliation charge by the boar.

The impending battle forced a tactical withdrawal by the Gurkhas, where they reformed and regrouped in the branches of the nearest trees. They had their superior fire power and skills gleaned during extensive training on the battlefields at Aldershot on their side. (And of course the battlefields in the Falklands, where it was reputed that leaflets were dropped on the Argies that said 'The Gurkhas are coming; they will silently slit your throats in the night whilst you sleep'. Yes, even the Argies knew of the Ghurkas' reputation about doing exactly that thing. Ooo! What nasty people, glad they're on our side. Of course, the whole idea was to stop the Argies going to sleep, so they would be too weary to fight.)

Anyway, back to my 'war correspondence'. When the boar tribe eventually realised that their losses were by now enormous and indeed, they were facing complete annihilation at the hands of the now re-organised and regrouped Gurkhas, they capitulated and beat a hasty retreat and melted back into the jungle.

By definition, the Gurkha is accomplished with his kukri in the butchery trade, and the vanquished and by now butchered boar were flown back by chopper to the messes at APC. And very nice they tasted too!

* * *

140

Not all trips into the jungle were so fruitful.

Before the Gurkhas started their tour, they were preceded by some Welsh regiment (I forget who). One of their patrols went into the jungle for their 'walk-about' and on the first night had set up their camp at one of the typical 'suitable' sites. They had set up their beds as instructed, viz off the ground to let the wildlife travel under and not over you; but not too high as to show a silhouette to the enemy. They had got a fire going and cooked their meal from the compo packs, and drunk their illicit and, by now, very warm beer that they had hidden in their packs. They settled down for the night after posting their first guard.

One of the group had made his bed about two feet off the ground and next to those trees that you have all seen pictures of, the ones where the roots come out of the trunk at all sorts of levels and then go into the ground.

He awoke in the night to find that his right arm felt rather heavy and he could not lift it. Our hero thought that he had perhaps got his hand trapped in one of the roots whilst he had been tossing and turning in the night thanks to his hot fizzy beer. He decided to try and pull his arm but he could not do that either.

He reached for his torch with his free hand so that he could see what the problem was. As soon as he turned on the torch he screamed and passed out.

The guy on guard wondered what the noise had been, and went bimbling over to his comrade to see. He shone his torch at our now comatose hero and promptly ran over to the patrol commander to wake him up.

'Corp, Corp, Dai has pushed his hand down a snake', he yells.

By now everyone is awake and discussing the situation. The best answer that came up was that this boa constrictor had been attracted to the smell of the camp and slithered over to see if anything would be good for him to eat. Dai meanwhile had let his arm flop over the side of his bed so that his hand was on the ground. The snake had come across this nice, fresh, warm lump of meat that seemed to be already dead and just lying there waiting to be eaten. Not one to miss out on such an opportunity, the snake promptly started to take the hand and then arm into its mouth. However, once the snake reached Dai's shoulder, it could not get any further.

Now, Boa Constrictors can only take food inwards, they cannot reverse the process, so poor old boa was now well and truly stuck.

The lads decided that for their first action they needed to prop open the snake's mouth with sticks to prevent further damage. Using a piece of string they measured Dai's other arm, added about six inches to be on the safe side, and with a machete, chopped off the back end of the snake. They then slit the snake and pulled it off.

Luckily for Dai, boas do not start to digest their food until they are asleep and the snake had been very much awake due to the unfortunate predicament it had found itself in. Therefore, Dai's arm had not been partially digested, though it was a funny colour, amongst other things.

Rumour had it that Dai was never quite the same after that. Some people are easily put off!

The third way to let down the old locks was with the good clean living things that everyone can do even when their wives are with them.

Here we all were in the Caribbean with the Florida Cayes, the second biggest barrier reef in the world, sitting just a couple of miles off the Belizean coast. Additionally, we all lived at what was also the country's main airport with the whole of the Americas on our route. There were two airlines based at the airport. However, the nicknames for the companies that ran them put many people off. One was called TACA and this one had been nicknamed 'Take A Chance Airways'. The other was SAHSA and nicknamed 'Stay At Home, Stay Alive'.

Because the camp was run by the grunts, the Air Force was told to provide the same recreational facilities as the grunts are used to all the time. (They do have some good points, even though they used to do five minutes of work/training per day and spend the rest of the day playing sports, which under grunt rules is the same as working. We on the other hand, worked a full eight-hour day maintaining kit.)

Anyway, what this meant was that at weekends we could sign out a Land-Rover, or whatever vehicle most suited our purposes, from MT and use it for recreation. We could go off camping, or exploring or whatever our little hearts desired.

The choppers, which belong to the army anyway but are run for them by the RAF, took a full load of people every weekend to one of the cayes. They always went to the same one.

Even the Harrier hides used to take it in turns to have a weekend off with the other hide on standby. The only people who used to work seven days per week were the chopper guys, who were ferrying folk to the cayes and trying to catch up with their work. (They were always at work, poor lads, they never seemed to get any time off.) Consequently the APC used to take on a deserted air about it at weekends, especially during the day. It miraculously came alive on the Saturday night for what was unkindly nicknamed by some as 'The Chimps Ball'.

Make no mistake about it, just like white girls, some of the black ones are beautiful and some are ugly and all sorts in between. I remember that Jock at Finningley had a simple philosophy when it came to the ladies. He always said that 'All women are beautiful, some more than others'. However, I, myself, personally, as my name sake at Swanton Morley always used to say, do not prescribe to that philosophy.

We would go out to the cayes by chopper at least twice in our tour, and to another one once or twice per month. There were hundreds of cayes, ranging from a 10 foot by 6 foot spit of sand that stuck out of the water by no more than an inch or two and with a solitary coconut palm tree in the middle, to a whole series of inhabited islands set up to trap the American tourist and make him part with his money. The biggest caye had a Brittan-Norman Islander aircraft as a ferry to the mainland and only cost 40 Belizean dollars. (3 Belize dollars to the pound at the time.)

Most people went out by water taxi to whichever caye they specified, and then spent the day there, and about once a month the whole weekend there. Every month our Flight would hire a big boat in advance, get down to the quay by three-tonner, which would be full of chicken and chops as our rations from the cook-house, and iceboxes full of beer from the mess, and motor out to one of the uninhabited cayes that would be about 200 feet long by 50 feet wide with enough palm trees to provide shade. We would set up the BBQ and get it alight using the husks of the coconuts that were always lying about in abundance as fuel. Everyone would do whatever they wanted, be it swimming, snorkelling, fishing or just paddling about in the water. If mangoes were on the caye and were ripe we used to have mango fights. We ended up covered in gopping mango slime, very few people actually ate them. It was easy to just leap into the sea to wash it all off afterwards.

The main advantage, of course, was that out on the cayes there was always a breeze which made the air very comfortable. This was a relief from APC, which, being surrounded by jungle, was always humid and therefore very sticky.

Our section had 'acquired' a Rigid Raider Marine Commando type boat with a small outboard engine.

We would go for a trundle up the river and explore some of the virgin jungle looking for wild bananas and pineapple. We knew what they looked like but did not dare risk any of the other exotic looking fruits that seemed to be in abundance. Sometimes, we would get chased back to the boat by monkeys, usually howler monkeys, but no doubt they were just curious. We didn't stop to find out. Monkeys can be very vicious.

One lazy afternoon we were puddling along in the boat through a very thick bit of jungle when I noticed something about ten feet in front of us in the water. I was steering at the time, and as I stood up to see what it was, at the same time this snake, that had been swimming across, lifted a head the size of a football to look at me.

It dived and I applied maximum power; this thing was the size of the Loch Ness monster. Whew, saved again!

One of the lads used to go down to the river that was at the side of one of the villages for a bit of a paddle and a cool off. He had noticed that all the local kids kept to the shallows and even the grown-ups would only swim at the edge. He had fancied one of the girls, so the next time that she was there he thought he would show off a bit. He dived into the water and swam to the other side of the river and then swam back again. As he got back, all the locals started clapping him.

He asked the girl why, and she said that his white skin must be magic, for if any of them had tried to swim across like that they would have been eaten by the alligators.

He got his girl but he never went in the river again.

Trips up country were popular. Just driving around to the various watering holes for a beer and into the hills to places on the touristy trail. Places like the 'Thousand Foot Falls' where the jungle changed to pine forest, compliments of the Royal Navy. They had planted them in the days when they had wooden ships as a source of softwood. By the time that the trees had grown to a useful size, the navy had changed to steel and didn't want pine anymore. Who would want pine when there is an abundance of rare and exotic hardwoods around?

Belize is in the area of Central America that was inhabited by the Mayan nation. Consequently, there are lots of Mayan settlements around and everyone visited at least one in their tour. There was one that had been cleared just to make it accessible, but then only with 4WD Land-Rover type vehicles. The local economy would not support any refurbishment at all. Many were still completely wild and some still remain to be discovered.

* * *

A Belizean home, complete with 'company car' (bike) on the drive

Harrier GR3 loading and the lorry used when 'in the field'

Every year the fly-boys have an allotment of full weight, drill, thousand pound bombs to drop. Due to the high cost, they were allocated something really generous, like six bombs per squadron per year.

Bearing in mind that the Harrier carried three as a standard war load, six bombs were not really adequate. It is possible to recover these bombs and refurbish them to use again as freebies. i.e. they did not come out of their ration of six if they were used again.

I decided to go to the range during one of the drops to assess the possibility of recovery. During the drops, a range safety officer and an army GLO worm (Ground Liaison Operator) would be dropped off at the range by chopper. The GLO worm incidentally was the grunt, who used to 'illuminate' the target with a laser beam so that the Harrier jockey's bomb sight could use this spot as an aiming point.

I arranged my lift with the choppers and all three of us did a precursory check of the range, where we discovered a horse stuck in the mud in one of the water filled bomb holes from some previous live bomb drop. We had a go at getting him out but to no avail. We fed him some greenery, as he was obviously starving, but by now the fly-boys were on their way.

We retired to the observation tower, hoping that the horse would not be hit as the aircraft were also doing gunnery and rocketry at the same time.

At the end of the day the horse had survived, but was by now even more frightened. We had another go at getting him out but still failed. I checked the bomb holes made by the fly-boys and found that they had already filled up with slimy mud. I decided that there was no way we could get the bombs out of the swampy range. By now the chopper was on its way to pick us up.

After we climbed aboard, we got the pilot to agree to land at the nearest village, much to the consternation, and then delight, of the villagers as we unloaded on to them all of our packed food (which included things like compo cheese, fizzy drinks, sweets and chocolate etc.). Any of our 'packed meals' that we did not eat we used to give to the kids who were always lining the road. We told the head honcho about the horse that was there for the taking. Horses would cost an average Belizean a lifetime's salary, so they should have been pleased.

When I checked with the GLO worm a few days later he told me that the horse was dead in the crater.

We used to use the range for demolition of Lifex (Life Expired) and U/S (Un-Serviceable) explosive components. We used to go out by chopper, blast away and then return. We were always being moaned at about the cost of using a chopper for this and it would appear that some years later they had tried to reduce this cost by travelling overland.

A guy called 'AJ' Smith related a tale to me that had happened to him when he was a Corporal, and his boss Nige (or 'Sarge' to his friends).

They had done all the usual planning and stuff, and had decided to go for a 'recce run' beforehand. They set off at six in the morning and intended to be back by evening. They took a few wrong turns in the jungle but eventually arrived at the site without any major problems, having managed to miss the swampy bits of their route. They did the good boy scout bit and cooked themselves a 'nourishing' (? – his words, not mine) meal from their compo packs, then decided that they had plenty of time to get back. However, within minutes of trying to do so, 'AJ' misjudged the track by, quote, a *mere* 20 cms, unquote, and the front axle disappeared into the swamp.

Choice Anglo Saxon expletives followed, but the lorry refused to jump out of the bog. They decided to spend the next four hours 'happily' engaged in trying to get as much wood as possible under the wheels in the bog and were relieved to find that the lorry managed to crawl out of its hole; no doubt spurred on by the gentle words of encouragement that were being whispered by our two intrepid heroes. (Or was it the threat of what would happen to it if it did not pull itself out?) Anyway, out they all came, but within minutes were in an even worse situation, when the whole of the lorry suddenly fell beneath the surface. This time there was no way that they were going to get it out.

To cut a long story short, they spent three days in the jungle desperately trying to remember everything that they had been taught in jungle survival classes. They started collecting water and hunting animals for food etc. etc. and thought that at some time, someone must realise that they were actually missing. However, as the route taken was not really an 'official' one (no route in the jungle could ever be 'official'), no-one knew where they were exactly. Neither did they have a radio. (I can imagine the conversation with our officer corps when they tried to obtain a radio, they would have been met with an incredulous 'What do you want a radio for?')

They were eventually met by MT's SWAMPY truck (a big crane on a 10-ton lorry especially designed for use in swamps), who managed to trace them from a 'fix' given to them by a passing chopper.

Whilst being towed out, Swampy also got stuck, and it too, was then pulled out by the four-tonner. This had the advantage of negating the fixed charge of a 'slab' whenever Swampy was called out to free someone's vehicle. A 'slab' by the way is a box of twenty-four tins of beer which formed a currency to pay for any small misdemeanours that people sometimes found they had committed, like being late for work, where the 'chief' would fine the culprit a slab instead of going through the nausea of the formal 252 (charge) procedure. The slab would be 'paid-in' to the section fund for the next 'beer-call'.

These two armourers learned a thing or two about jungle survival from that episode, especially to fill any available spare space with water cans.

I and some friends had already spent a long weekend over the Easter break, across the border in Mexico at a place called Chetumal. Very civilised, the buildings had windows, which is more than could be said for Belize. Everywhere in Belize had windows made from fly screen and that was all.

For my two weeks R&R, I had decided to go to Florida with John, one of my armourers from the hide. We flew off to Miami and caught the old greyhound to Kissimee, which is the home of Disneyworld and the Epcot Centre. After spending five days doing the old 'rubber-necking' bit, we decided to go our separate ways as we wanted different things from henceforth.

I hired a car from 'Rent-a-wreck' (the car was brand new by the way with only about 500 miles on the clock) and drove up the Eastern Seaboard to a town called 'Jackson' (had to really, didn't I?), across to the western side and then drove back down again to eventually cut across to Miami.

It was on the western side, in the swamps, that I called in a bar for a beer before trying to find some accommodation for the night. I got chatting to the barmaid who noticed eventually that I was 'not from around here-about's'. I had put on my best plum accent for her benefit when she said 'Gee, ah ain't never screwed no Englishman afore', so I did my cultural bit and obliged the good lady. She saved me two nights' board and lodging, and she could drink more beer than I could and still remain standing. Luckily, she provided all the beer.

Came the end of my tour, and it had been decided by 'the management' that posts like mine would have a week's overlap of personnel to give a decent hand-over. Jack, my replacement, arrived and we did what everyone does with new arrivals, viz took him down town to prevent him going to sleep. It was the best way to get the body clock sorted out, bearing in mind that Belize was some six hours behind UK.

We all took Jack, and another guy who had arrived on the same kite, down to do the rounds of all the usual haunts in Belize city. We went into one of the more seedy joints and were drinking quite well. A group of girls were shaking their ample bosoms in time with the music and I pointed them out to Jack. He gave me a very distasteful look.

At that point, the girls noticed us looking at them and came over. One of them came behind me, slid one hand in my shirt and the other down the waistband of my trousers, and said 'Hey white man, I wanna fuck your body.'

At this point, Jack fled.

I had already had my check with the 'Dick Doctor' and received a clean bill of health prior to my return to UK, so I was not going to risk it all for a bonk. We all went to look for Jack, who, it transpired, was a God-fearing Bible-punching armourer (I didn't know such a thing existed) who now realised that his mission in life was to change the ways of this heathen nation.

'Oh dear,' thinks I. 'This guy is going to have a problem.'

I saw him about four years later and he said that he had hated Belize. I also saw some of the lads who I had left behind under his control and they said that they had hated him with a passion. He had, apparently, tried to put a curfew on them going off camp, and other 'party pooper' things.

In the Armament Role bay was my corporal, who was called Mick. He had been having problems with his wife, and things did not look too promising for the marriage after his return. It had been like that since day one of his tour in Belize. For his R&R he had gone to Washington DC and had met this girl. He later said to me, and others, that on the flight home to UK he was going to jump ship in Washington and stay with the girl.

I gave him the counselling bit, saying that he would be arrested for desertion and brought back to UK anyway. You know how these young lads have their brains in their dicks at that age (just like I had been) and he had been given a 'good time' in Washington.

I arranged with the boss, without explaining the reason why, to get him on the same return flight to UK with me. I arranged with another 'chief' who was also going home, that when we landed at Washington to refuel (we were 'let out' by the customs people for the couple of hours that we were there), one of us was to be with him for every second. We had forewarned him that there was no way he was going to jump the wall. We even trailed him to the loo.

I don't know whether he ever forgave us, or indeed, if we did the right thing in preventing him, but it seemed right at the time.

Something that they didn't warn us about until it was too late was the MEDALERT card. During our clearance from the unit, the Medical Centre gave us a MEDALERT card that stated:

> WARNING – The bearer of this card has been in Belize. Should any lumps or nodules form on the skin, they may be CUTANEOUS LEISHMANIASIS. Contact the Institute of Tropical Medicine for advice.

There we all were, a danger to World Health. Who says so? WHO says so, that's who! (WHO is the World Health Organisation, just in case someone out there didn't know that.)

I applied for my posting and asked to go somewhere either close to my house (Coningsby, Lincolnshire) or close to my boys in Oxford.

I was posted to Honington in Suffolk.

One hundred miles from my house and one hundred miles from my boys.

Gee thanks Innsworth, starred again! (Innsworth is the Personnel Management Centre for the RAF and prides itself on posting people to where they want to go, Ha!)

14

RAF HONINGTON

(Boredom Unlimited)

I had taken my trusty Merc out of its temporary storage during my disembarkation leave, and had resurrected my relationships with Fay and Jennie, therefore spending time with them at 'their place'.

Fay still wanted my baby and kept supplying me with the dates that would be best for her to conceive. She kept promising, and providing, all sorts of sexual delights, if I would go and spend the night with her over those 'special' periods.

No, I don't suppose that 'period' is the right word to use there, I suppose I should just say 'days', or rather 'nights'!

Jennie in the meantime had applied for a teaching job with the BFES (British Forces Education Service) in Germany.

I decided that I needed some sort of base in Oxford to enable me to see my sons. Driving all that way just to spend an afternoon walking around Oxford city centre with them was not a lot of fun, especially as I then had to drive back again.

To enable some of my influence to wash off required that we spend as much time together as possible, and preferably spending periods living together, albeit only for weekends or holidays, was in my view, essential. I considered all the options, which were to buy a flat or a residential caravan in Oxford or to buy a boat to keep on the Thames. Flats were very expensive, as indeed is all property down there, and caravans were too boring. Well, a boat it had to be then.

I was quite flush with cash after my Belize tour, and I purchased a 28-foot four-berth cabin cruiser with a BMC diesel engine. It was a Seamaster 813, which I named 'Phantom Phixer' after my time on the old tomb. We would now be able to tootle about on the river to our hearts content and went both upstream and downstream as far as was navigable.

151

Boats are, funnily enough, classified by customs and excise as agricultural vehicles, which meant that any diesel fuel that we bought was of the pink duty free variety. That fact helped to keep the cost down but unfortunately the cost of anything to do with boating is horrendously expensive. It was over £100 per year for a licence to use the boat on the water, £150 per year for insurance and £700 per year for mooring fees in Oxford.

After my disembarkation leave had come to an end, I rolled up at Honington at the appointed time and took an instant dislike to the place. For a start, it was Tornado aircraft, and for a second, the mess was a dump.

After speaking to a couple of singlies in the bar I discovered that we, as singlies, and paying for our food and accommodation, could opt to live at a cheaper rate, in a wooden hut 'hidden' away from everyone. We each had two rooms: a bedroom and sitting room. Oh well, stuff the mess! I would just use it to eat in and treat the hut as if I was at home.

My first day at work revealed that I was to be in charge of the Gun Bay, Small Arms and ASF Armourers. The ASF Armourers had a Sergeant, and as I knew zilch about Tornado anyway (I never did the Tornado course) there was nothing to do there except 'seat indies' (Independent Checks).

Small Arms had a Sergeant, so all I needed to do was the 'weekly check' (weekly count of weapons as a double check over and above the count that the Sergeant did every day).

The 27 mm Mauser guns (history lesson – named after Peter von Mauser, 1838–1914, and his brother Wilhelm, 1834–1882, who set up the company after first inventing a new type of pistol) were not being fired as they had not yet been given their 'Release to Service' (not authorised to be fired as all safety and other testing had not been completed), so all that was being done in the gun bay was anti-deterioration maintenance (yawn), and in any case had a Sergeant to run it.

What in tarnation was I supposed to do?

After the first week I was bored to tears with work and decided that I had to get away. The rest could sit on their bums twiddling their thumbs but not me. For them, Parkinson's Law (work expands so as to fill the time available for its completion) was the order of the day!

I might add at this juncture that I am lambasting second line only here. The guys on the Squadrons were established just like any other Squadron and were as busy as ever with their 'crisis management' style of management. My old mate Jack Mcmenamin was the Trade Manager on TWCU (Tornado Weapons Conversion Unit; just like a Squadron but bigger) and he was always desperate for manpower. I remember a tale he told me when 'Tonkas' (Tornados) were first introduced into service. It goes as follows:

One fine day, when the Lothian and Borders traffic police were out on the Berwickshire moors, with their newly acquired Radar Speed-trap Gun, they were happily engaged in booking speeding motorists, when their kit locked up, took a reading of over 600 mph and then promptly exploded in a fizz of acrid smoke. One second later the mystery was explained when a Tornado from the TWCU hurtled over their heads at about 50 feet above ground. Mr Plod was so upset about the damage to their toy that they complained to the RAF. They were somewhat upset when the reply from the Air Force stated that the police had been very lucky, as the aircraft's radar had 'locked on' to an enemy radar, and had triggered an automatic retaliatory Air-to-Surface missile attack. Luckily, missiles had not actually been fitted to the aircraft.

Not only did I decide to get away from Honington, but also that I should get the post dis-established. Needless to say I did not make myself popular by going around and encouraging everyone to get their post dis-established also.

I used to upset the Flight Sergeant something rotten, when I told him that his job should be done by a Corporal. He used to go red in the face, fit to blow a blood vessel. Still, like most of the second line SNCO armourers at Honington, he had lots of time to sit down and write what a wonderful job everyone (except me of course) was doing.

It was a case of everyone scratching everyone else's back and promotion was phenomenal; they all got promoted. My stance ensured that I was not going to get promoted but my conscience was clear.

The Corporals and below of course were doing the same job as any of them would do anywhere, but I blame the Officer Corps and most of the SNCOs for hiding what I considered to be a disgraceful situation.

During this phase of being somewhat fed up, I wrote an article entitled 'A Tale of Three Chiefs' for the Station Magazine that, due to its contentious nature, I did not think would get published. However, it did and the next issue of the magazine included an article from one of the squadrons that also asked for the author of the article to produce some more, as it had kept 13 Squadron ground-crew in arguments for a month.

The article in question was a muted complaint about the way that the service victimises single people. It was published as follows:

A Tale of Three Chiefs.

Once upon a time, three chiefs all worked in the same office doing a similar job. They all bought their own house in the area, so as to provide a stable home life for their families. They all lived the same distance away from their office. Two of the chiefs received money for travelling expenses but the third chief was not allowed to claim. Often, all three chiefs would travel to other offices around the country and spend a few days at a time talking to people. The first two chiefs used to get free food and accommodation but the third had to pay. Eventually, all three chiefs were posted. The first was posted 125 miles away, and decided to continue living in his own house. He was paid so much in travel expenses that he used the money to buy, tax and insure one of the new 100 mpg diesel engine cars. The second was posted 450 miles away. He decided to live at his new office and was given free accommodation and almost free food. His children were at boarding school (paid for by the people at the office) just a few miles from his new office, so he was able to see them regularly. He was also given extra travel warrants and extra pay as well, so that he could go and see his wife who was looking after his house. The third chief was posted 90 miles from his house, but because he could not claim travelling expenses like the first chief, he could not afford to travel daily from his house, especially as he had a wife and children to support. He therefore had to live in at his new office just like the second chief. However, he could not get free accommodation and almost free food like the second chief, he had to pay the full amount just like the single men who live in and didn't have a family to support.

What sort of fairy tale is this? Would any organisation penalise the third chief and yet go out of its way to be as helpful as possible by offering cash incentives to the first two chiefs? All three chiefs financially support their wives and children and wish to provide their families with a stable home. What then is the difference? In a word – wife. The third chief has an ex wife. His children do not live with him but that is obviously not of major importance, as the children of the second chief do not live with him either. Seemingly, the third chief is blanket categorised as a single man even though he financially supports his children and ex wife. Is anyone prepared to stand up for the minority of divorced men or could it be that the policy makers, or at least those who have the policy makers' ears, are entirely biassed towards married men, being married themselves. Divorced men are still family men and still supporting a wife and children.

NOTE; Taking into account travel cost, separation, food, boarding school (2 children) etc., the extra annual financial burden on the RAF, is £1800 for chief one and £6900 for chief two' (1986 fiscal year).

Night-life in the Bury St Edmunds area turned out to be pretty good. I had discovered the local 'singlies' club where I discovered that for some reason, and much to my delight, I was very popular with the ladies. I almost found it embarrassing at times to find all these women vying for my attention. I had always tried to ensure that the Merc did not become a 'pull', so I used to park well away from the club and walk in. I had been permanently surrounded by these three attractive ladies, long before they knew of the car.

It transpired that one of them, Susan, lived on my route from 'Honny' to 'St Ed's', and she asked if I would give her a lift in to the club (it was after that when the three of them found out about the car). That night, when I took her home, she invited me in for coffee and, as her daughter was watching TV, led me into the bedroom where she promptly started to seduce me.

Now, it is very easy for a woman to seduce a man. All she has to do is let him know that she wants to seduce him and she has. If a fellah thinks enough about a woman to take her home, he certainly thinks enough about her to want to bed her.

Isn't life easy for women?

Susan became my sort of 'regular' (favourite position – standing up), but I was still under the constant attention of the other two, Helen (favourite position – doggy fashion) and Ann (favourite position – missionary).

I would see the three of them on a regular basis. Additionally, I would see another from the club on a sort of 'as they come' basis, and I was still travelling to my house at weekends so the 'Boston and Skeggy' connection was still maintained.

One particular occasion I remember was when I climbed out of bed with Susan and went to see Helen. After finishing making love with Susan, I was in bed making love with Helen, after only nineteen minutes, 15 of those spent travelling.

Not bad, not bad at all!

What this meant was that during my time at 'Honny', there were six women that I was sleeping with, so I do have some fond memories of the place. It's a good job work was so slack, I could walk around like a zombie all day long to recover.

I had put it around that I wanted out from 'Honny' so much that the boss of the Armament Engineering Flight at CSDE (Central Servicing Development Establishment) heard about it. He rang me up and asked if I was the guy who used to be in the Phantom AEDIT at big C. Apparently he knew of my work from there; he used to be at HQSTC at the time, and sat next to the guy that I did most of my work for.

After confirming that I was, he asked me if I would like a posting to the CSDE detached flight at RAE (Royal Aircraft Establishment) Farnborough. I jumped at the chance, I knew that I would not be able to continue with my sex life at this hectic pace for much longer so a posting would provide me with the ideal opportunity to say 'bye and thanks' to the ladies in the Suffolk area.

The guy who, on paper, came in to replace me, did not fill my chair but went to work elsewhere. (In the Bomb Dump in fact.) At least I had convinced them of that bit. I was gratified to learn that one year later the bubble had burst and the establishment was drastically reduced.

Spoof picture of the weapons that could be fitted to the old 'string-bag' that we had at Swanton Morley

15

RAE FARNBOROUGH

(Attack Weapons Division)

Before going to Farnborough, it was agreed that I would spend six weeks at the home of CSDE at Swanton Morley in Norfolk to learn about the CSDE way of doing things, and to make contact with the guys that I would be working and dealing with, albeit it at the end of a phone.

Swanton Morley was unique in the Air Force in that it consisted of a thousand or so SNCO engineers plus a few others who are always required to run any typical RAF camp, like cooks, pencil pushers, Medics, blanket stackers, MT and the like. The aim of the CSDE was primarily to cover the introduction of new equipment into service and engineering support to anyone, about anything, at any time. It also had its own set of rules about things and its own way of doing things.

I discovered that my job at Farnboro' would be the introduction into service of the Tucano aircraft escape system, the introduction into service of the Tornado FII Sky Flash Missile Launcher and NATO Interoperability. Additionally, I was to act as an advisor to the RAE (Royal Aircraft Establishment) on an 'as and when' basis.

They were a good bunch of lads in the flight at Swanton, and I spent a lot of my time with Jim Smith who introduced me to the dreaded ICR Procedure (Inception Reporting Procedure, don't ask me why there is a 'C' in the abbreviation; I told you CSDE had its own set of rules). ICRs were the main mechanism, the main 'tool' as it would be called these days, to enable the introduction of new kit to be achieved satisfactorily. ICRs were already extant for the Launcher but I would have to start from scratch for the seat ones.

NATO Interoperability was a new one on me, but it entailed producing the relevant publication, a topic 12B-CL, to enable RAF guys to fit RAF weapons to foreign Air Force aircraft and vice versa. Most of the foreign weapons were of US manufacture, so I got to know them quite well.

A guy in the flight called Pete Gilbert was also a singlie and he introduced me to the 'crumpet factories' in that 'Bootiful' city of Norwich. Quite a swinging town, oops sorry, city, is Norwich. (They get upset if you call their 'Fine City' a town.) Not at all the sleepy hollow that I would have associated with this neck of the woods.

Now Pete Gilbert was a bit of a lady-killer, he was around 53 years of age but looked 35 and was as fit as a 25 year old. All in all, I hated him! (Only joking Pete, honest!)

At one of the local singlies bars, in Dereham actually, he introduced me to Shona, who was a bubbly little blonde. After we had the usual couple of nights of straight sex, I discovered that what she really loved was oral sex. That was her giving me oral sex, not the other way round, particularly. I did not complain! She knew that we would not continue our relationship, once I got down to Farnboro. I had been dropping hints that it would be unrealistic for me to travel back at weekends, and things like that, so she reluctantly accepted the fact that once I got to Farnborough, then that would be that. She was still giving me those rather lovely blow-jobs though.

Over the last weekend, and just a couple of days before I was due to drive away, she asked me if I would go with her to her friend's house for a barbecue. She forewarned me that her friend's husband had just run off with another MAN, so she was not sure how she would react to me. It hits a woman hard enough when their hubby runs off with another woman, but it hits them even harder when they discover that he actually prefers another man to her.

What the hell, of course I would go, I'm a big boy now!

Off we went in the afternoon and sat in the garden eating all the usual barbie fare. I had only said a cursory 'hello' to the woman (Jackie) and left it at that, whilst I drank her (or her ex husband's) beer.

Shona said that the food and beer was making her feel randy (heaven only knows why, it makes me feel sleepy) and off she trots to see her friend. Upon her return, she informs me that Jackie had said it was OK for us to go up and use her bed. Very obliging, I thought, I could do with a sleep, so off we went. (I didn't get the chance of a sleep though.)

When we came back down again, most of the other guests had gone and dusk was settling in. I settled down to drink the remainder of the beer, just so that Jackie would not have the trouble of having to put it back in the fridge you understand.

Jackie came and sat next to me and said that she was sorry that she had been so cool towards me. She then started to ask me things like 'would I continue to see Shona'. I put her in the picture on that score. She then started to explain about puffy hubby, and that she had never known any other men but him, he had been a childhood sweetheart apparently. I gave her all the right soothing and reassuring phrases like 'It's his loss', and 'Throw yourself in at the deep end like Shona had done', and 'do all the things that you have only fantasised about' and things like that.

She thought about this for a while and then said, 'I have always wanted to know how women's pussies differ.'

I must admit that this came as quite a shock, this was my first conversation with her and she comes out with something like that. I took a while to explain this to her in graphic detail and I said that she and Shona should go off and compare notes; but if they did, could I watch. I must admit that I said the last bit half jokingly, but I was not joking. I didn't really fancy Jackie all that much but the thought of this erotic experience got my blood pressure going.

I settled into that nice soporific doze that one does after a few beers and a barbie and a bonk, and awoke to find that I was on my own. I wandered into the house to find the two girls sitting on the floor and watching a blue movie video, which unfortunately was nearly finished. I asked them what they had been doing, apart from watching the video.

'Comparing notes" came the reply.

'About what?' I ask.

'Pussies.'

I told them that I was disappointed that I had not had an invite to give my expert opinion, but asked them what the notes showed.

'We are completely different.'

Damn! This was a missed opportunity and I was getting nowhere. We all settled down to watch the news on the TV and Jackie provided even more food. By about the time that I was going to suggest to Shona that we go home, she came over to me and sat on my knees, facing me with one leg either side of mine. She lifted her skirt and I could see that she had removed her knickers (or maybe she had never put them back on again).

Jackie walked out of the room.

Shona unzipped me and relieved my manhood from the restraint of my trousers. I said 'What about Jackie'? Meaning, quite obviously to me, that she may come back in the room and catch us.

'She can wait her turn,' says Shona.

In walks Jackie and comes over to where we are, with me hastily trying to hide John Thomas from view.

'Don't stop,' she says.

I let Shona take him out again and the next thing that I know is that Jackie is being instructed by Shona in the fine art of giving a man a blow-job, and I was the lucky recipient. We all eventually ended up in bed and I screwed them both. I also gave them a description, from my vantage point, of how their pussies differed.

That was a night of pure debauchery, I am pleased to say.

I had been sent off on a visit to see my predecessor, Ben Franklin, who was leaving the Air Force and going to work for the company that was producing the Sky Flash Missile Launcher for us. He had been working with them for the past five years or so and was now off to join them as an employee.

Ben did all the usual handover type things and we did the circuit of as many people as possible that I would be dealing with during my tour. I also took the opportunity to sort out some lodgings in the area as all singlie 'non comms' lived in 'digs' whilst the Officers lived in the Officers' Mess at Farnboro'.

I had previously put an advert in the local rag that read:

'Non smoking, single, RAF SNCO posted to RAE requires lodgings.'

To my utter amazement, I received 68 replies.

I intended that whilst at Farnboro', I would cycle to and from work, so my first filter of responses was to 'bin' the ones that were either too near or too far away. That knocked the number down to 22.

Nothing for it but to visit them all, so I arranged loads of appointments. Some were very expensive and some were very cheap. It was obvious after only a few visits that the prospective landlords had no real idea of what their accommodation was worth. It was also obvious that some of the female prospective landlords (err, landladies, err landpersons or whatever) were offering more than lodgings. Whilst the thought of that interested the man in me, I could foresee future problems in a relationship like that. Anyway, some of them were married.

I ended up with what was almost the cheapest of the bunch but definitely offered the best accommodation. The room was large, light, quiet and the owners were a couple who were close to retirement and lived on their own. As it happened, they treated me like a son when I moved in some three weeks later and I spent some of my best times with Kit and Arthur.

Work was enjoyable, and I had my own office in AW Div. (Attack Weapons Division) in building T70, which was on the far side of the airfield. I was the only member of the RAF in the building, which was full of civilian research type folk. They would pop in for a chat, primarily to ask me how the RAF might act given some particular situation or what, out of a number of options, would be our preference and they would also bring in some draft specifications that they were preparing for me to comment on.

My claim to fame is that I introduced into the 'specs', the need for equipment to be engineered such that special tools were not required. We all know the situation of going on detachment having to take tons of special tools with us 'just in case' they might be needed.

On the other side of the airfield was the IAM (Institute of Aviation Medicine) and a CSDE detached flight of 'comms' guys (Air Wireless Fitters as they used to be known).

Whenever I felt the need for service type company, I would peddle over to the Comms guys for a coffee and a chat. Bearing in mind that they were 'fairies' they were a pretty good bunch of lads.

My admin was done by the IAM and my boss was 120 miles away. All in all, I was pretty much my own boss, but I did phone back to Swanton to let them know where I would be the following week. I could arrange to go where ever I wanted, at any time without having to fill in the reams of paperwork that had to be signed by at least four people, like everyone else had to do at Swanton. That was a definite advantage. Good job that I am a conscientious sort, 'cos the system could have easily been open to abuse.

The Sky Flash Missile Launcher was just about finally developed, and all that I had to do was the test set.

The Tucano was being introduced by a CSDE PT (Project Team) based at Shorts in Belfast (Project Team joke; What is the propeller on the Tucano for? Answer, to keep the pilot cool; if you don't believe that then just turn the engine off in flight and watch the pilot sweat). The ICR system that they were using was a computer based 'one off' that was supposed to be the pilot for all future ICRs. It transpired that I would

161

be looking after both 'on' and 'off' aircraft aspects of the escape system so I ended up by also being a part time member of the PT. This meant that I would have to fly out to Belfast on a regular basis to input my ICRs onto the database and attend meetings and trials as required.

Luckily, the admin for this was easy. All that I had to do was to phone the IAM admin office to give them the dates and that was it, no paperwork whatsoever on my part. When they phoned me back with the flight details, I would arrange a lift to Heathrow with one of the comms guys, pick up my ticket, fly out to Aldergrove, find the covert office to ring MT to come and pick me up and take me to the mess.

As 'the troubles' were at their height at the time, everything was covert. The PT lived at Aldergrove in married quarters or the mess but drove every day in an MT-supplied covert vehicle to Shorts. MT used to buy the vehicles secondhand from a local car auction and then sell them on again after a couple of months, that way it would make it difficult for the 'baddies' to latch on to covert vehicles.

All the usual security measures (like never getting into a black London taxi cab in Belfast, as they were nicknamed 'IRA Staff Cars' for obvious reasons) were in place which, for even more obvious reasons, I will not divulge, but we did try to comply with most of them.

Lots of areas were 'no go' for us, but quite often we would drive down the forbidden Falls Road just as part of our route variation, and things like that. Sometimes we would get diverted into some very dodgy places due to bomb scares or riots or something similar.

I remember once we were working a bit of overtime and Neil and I drove in to work on a Saturday morning. We got diverted into a Republican area because of some rioting where some shots had been fired on the route of the Orange Order parade. We pulled into a side street to let them pass, hoping that gunmen were not in that street waiting for the parade. Just before it reached us the band started to play. It struck up the Beatles song 'We all live in a yellow submarine', which both Neil and I found to be somewhat incongruous and we both promptly fell about laughing.

Maybe that is what the riot was about; they were complaining about the choice of music.

One of the lads on the PT was a singlie by the name of Dusty Miller. As everyone else on the team and two of the members who were living in the mess were married, he used to look forward to me arriving as he then had someone that he could go off camp with in the evenings.

There were lots of areas that we could not go to and of course, everything was covert. We had to book-out and book-in at camp and we also were supposed to inform them exactly where we were going. Needless to say, as we didn't know ourselves where we were going until we got there, we used to give them some nice 'safe' location as our destination. Dusty knew where all the 'no go' areas were anyway, but we had a fairly wide area of choice. We kept to all the safe pubs.

One night we went to a British Legion club. The place was like Fort Knox. It was obviously in a safe area, but even so was surrounded by concrete blocks with more at the ends of every street that led to it. It was in a compound behind a twenty-foot high fence, with the whole area illuminated by floodlights and scanned by security cameras. The entrance was first through a metal detector arch and then to a single person filter system where once you were in you could not get either any further in or back out again until released by the security man.

This is where protestants go for a nice quiet drink of an evening! Makes us appreciate the good old English country pub.

We flashed our RAF identity cards, and were welcomed like the prodigal son. No sooner had we got inside than we were having drinks bought for us. Everyone soon discovered who the strangers were, due to the fact that they announced us over the tannoy. We had to stand up to be recognised and they all gave us a welcoming clap. (Clapping of hands I mean, I didn't mean they gave us the other sort of 'clap'.)

Even more important, a couple of girls came over to join us. We got on pretty well with them, but were un-eased when they recounted some friendly tales from past evenings. It appears that one night, some other young girls had been in the club, and at the end of the evening, when 'God Save The Queen' started to be played, the new girls had not sprung to attention quick enough. At the end of 'The Queen', the girls were promptly beaten up by the rest of the women.

Needless to say, we listened intently for the opening bars of that well known tune, and kept an eye open on everyone around us; any sign of hasty movement and we would be ramrod straight quicker than any drill sergeant could have taught us.

When the moment for 'The Queen' did arrive, we must have passed with flying colours, 'cos we were not attacked at the end of it. Unless of course they forgave us because we had taken the Queen's shilling and were therefore exempt; a bit like the Fish Heads (Royal Navy) who still toast the queen whilst sitting down.

We took the girls home but made a detour to a bit of waste land beforehand. It was freezing cold outside so we could not disappear into the shadows to try our luck, but we did end up with sticky fingers though; better than nowt.

The rules that were imposed on servicemen who intended to chat up a girl in Northern Ireland were almost impossible to comply with. Before meeting the girl for the second time, the fellah had to obtain loads of 'relevant' details about her, report those details to security, who would then vet her and finally give clearance to see her later.

Imagine the scene.

Boy meets girl for very first time. 'Hello, my name is Dave. Please tell me your full name, date of birth, full address, your religion, your political views, and lots of other details that I have listed on this piece of paper. I will then go away, but I may be able to continue to chat you up in a month's time after I have been given clearance.' Yeah, Yeah!

No wonder the lads sat in their rooms watching telly.

When I had first arrived at Farnboro', I met a very petite lady called Janine. I would go to her house and she would get me playing with the kids for a few minutes before she sent them off to bed. After the arrival of the baby-sitter, we would go out somewhere for a drink. When we got back she would send the baby-sitter away and we would usually make love on the settee (she seemed to have some sort of rapport with that settee) and then we would go to bed. The next morning I had breakfast with her and the kids.

It then became apparent that she always had an excuse not to see me at weekends. The first couple of weekends I put down to the fact that she had something else arranged or perhaps just wanted the weekend to spend with her kids. One evening I asked her whether she would spend a weekend with me on the boat.

She said, in a quite matter of fact voice, that she could not do that or ever see me over the weekends, as that was when her husband came home.

Gulp!

She explained that her husband worked in Glasgow during the week and flew down every weekend. (He was a pilot and thumbed a lift each weekend back to Heathrow for free.) He had a flat and girlfriend in Glasgow and he also knew about me and her, and had said 'Good Show'.

I said 'Good bye'.

164

That was what they called an open relationship, but no way was I going to screw some other man's wife, even if he did approve. I had that done to me and I did not approve. I didn't need that complication in my life.

I then met another very petite lady by the name of Rosemary. Her name was not really Rosemary as she was Belgique, but she had anglicised her name from whatever it was in French. She had this huge mane of yellow blonde hair (natural, I found out soon after!) and, whilst she was quite tiny in stature, was very well endowed. She told me that after she and her husband had split up, I was the first one to sleep in her bed.

She did not need teaching in any of the finer points of humping but, not to put too fine a point on it, she was an alcoholic.

At first I suppose it seemed a novelty, because she was loaded and kept buying me prezzies and things and plying me with booze. However, the novelty soon wore off.

I quickly replaced Rosy with yet another petite (this must have been my petite phase) but dark haired and also very well endowed nurse called Wendy.

Now she had a very pleasant trait in her character, in that whenever she was touching me, she would be ever so gently stroking at the same time. Just moving her fingers, wherever her fingers happened to be resting at the time. She worked in the children's ward at the hospital, and said that she had picked up the habit whilst trying to soothe them. She said that it always worked, and within minutes they would be asleep. As she was very tactile by nature, her hand was always somewhere on my body, and all the time stroking. Mostly, not even aware that she was doing it.

Lovely!

I spent about two years or more with Wendy, and we became quite close. However, I did not move in with her as I would have then lost my lodging allowance, but we did spend a lot of time together and I was still able to see the boys regularly.

Lodging allowance was a lot of money and I had built up quite a nice little sum. Wendy and I had planned to buy a 'Granny Farm' (Retirement home) as she was a SRN (State Registered Nurse) and it is a legal requirement to have a SRN qualified nurse on the staff of a granny farm. I could have done all the property maintenance and general tinkering around, so it ought to have been a viable proposition.

However, I was not in love with her, so fought shy of going any further than just making tentative plans.

NATO Interoperability was an interesting aspect of my job and more and more tasks were given to me.

As 'interop' was mainly carried out in the NATO Central Region, i.e. Germany and surrounding countries, then the job entailed lots of travel to one of the units in the region. I would then go with a team from an RAFG unit to the base that would be supplying the aircraft.

For example, when I wrote the schedule for the Fighting Falcon F16 aircraft that could land at Wildenrath during a war scenario, to be re-armed with British weapons, then I would travel to Belgium, Holland and a USAF base in Germany. These were the nations that had been designated to fly into Wildenrath, and had to be visited, to initially gather information on the aircraft. (Yes, as far as the weapons aspects and pylons/carriers/release systems are concerned, they are almost different aircraft.)

I would then return to the UK to draft the schedule. Then, another return to Germany, to obtain initial validation from the host nation, and to carry out a 'hands on' verification of the schedule. This may then throw up the need for more visits.

This was a minimum of six separate trips to Germany. Each trip would require a week (drive to the unit on Monday and back again on the Friday so it was only three days on task) and the shuttle aircraft only flew to Germany on a Friday or a Monday, which meant that I had to fly out on the preceding Friday and return the Monday following our return to whichever unit I had travelled with.

Now you may remember that whilst I was at Coningsby, Jennie had applied for a teaching job in Germany and she had been successful. She was now teaching at Rheindahlen and had her own flat just outside Wildenrath.

How convenient!

I used to fly out on the Friday, spend the weekend with Jennie, travel with the team somewhere in Europe during the week, back by the Friday to the flat to spend another weekend with Jennie again, and then fly back on the Monday to the waiting arms of Wendy. I had it made!

This went on for almost all of my three years and, as I was going to Germany a minimum of about five or six times per year, I was building up a nice supply of 'duty free' as well.

All good things come to an end and this post was no exception. One of our Wing Commanders decided that he did not want any of his men

Visitors at Wildenrath for NATO Interoperability meeting

anywhere other than Swanton Morley, no matter what benefit the service gained by having them elsewhere.

As expected, he would not listen to reason; he was a Wing Commander, so of course he knew best! He actually cost the Air Force a lot of money in the short term, and a loss of engineering expertise in the long term. Needless to say he was promoted to Group Captain.

Give the Officer Corps enough string and they will destroy the RAF, the enemy within!

Every time that I had been on a visit back to base at Swanton Morley, my heart would sink as soon as I started to get close. As I drove through the gates I would be really depressed, even a few beers in the mess would not make the hurt go away.

In the early days when I returned to Swanton during my three-monthly visit, I would go and see Shona and spend the night with her, but eventually she found someone else so I stopped going. Just goes to show how fickle some women are!

Now I was actually being posted (effectively anyway) in to this horrible place. Time for a few changes! I sold the Merc, sold the boat and bought a new Ford Fiesta Diesel.

All I had to do now was to pack my worldly goods into the back and see what fate had in store for me.

16

RAF SWANTON MORLEY

(*The 'Mortuary'*)

As I drove through the gates of Swanton Morbid (one of the many uncomplimentary nicknames for this famous, or perhaps infamous, RAF camp) my heart sank even more than it had on any of my previous visits.

This time I was here for keeps, or at least for a period of time that had yet to be determined. I had been forewarned that I would probably be 'screened' (an administrative system which prevented me from being posted for any reason except promotion) for three years.

Three years I would have to spend in this pinnacle of bureaucratic nausea. Three years of spending half of my time wasted, in raising stupid bits of paper nonsense, that the Officer Corps had dreamed up for us to do, so as to keep them all in jobs. It was supposed to provide accountability and a management aid so that the Officer Corps knew what was happening. Fat chance! As is often said in the mob 'Roll on death, de-mob is too far away.'

All paperwork had to be produced in triplicate at the very least, signed by everyone and his dog, at least a year in advance (I exaggerate that last bit slightly) and with everyone in the management chain trying their best to dream up feeble excuses to prevent us from doing our job.

Why, the very first thing that happened when a new task came in to the unit, was that the paperwork went to the Group Captain and a Squadron Leader and his team of jolly helpers who were dedicated to try their very darndest to find as many reasons as possible why the task should be rejected.

Many a time a task sponsor would ring us up, from the Ministry say, asking how we were getting on with a particular task, and we would have to tell him that we had not even seen it yet, as it was still with the station master for consideration whether we should do it or not. Embarrassing!

Even though the task may have been authorised and signed by a Group Captain at the MoD, our own Group Captain had to 'accept' it. Power games senior officers play, and for no-one's benefit except their own. I concluded long ago that once an officer reached the rank of Squadron Leader and above, all they were interested in was scoring points over their contemporaries. The needs of the service came a distinct second place to their needs to score points so that they could be promoted to the dizzy heights.

The reason for this of course was to ensure that their pensions would keep them in luxury for the rest of their lives. Sybarites! The officer corps kept an eye on their pension from the first day of joining the service, whilst the rest of us only considered our pensions in the last couple of years of our long careers.

In the Air Force, the 'Peter Principle' (in any hierarchy, everyone tends to rise to the highest level of their incompetence) does not apply to the Officer Corps; they start off as incompetent and become even more so with seniority. It was certainly not useful to the Air Force having the hob-nobs bickering over who should do the work. By the time that the arguments finished we could have had the task over and finished. It used to make me really angry. (Bet you never guessed that, did you?)

To cap it all, the room that I had been graciously provided with in the mess was tiny, dull, dingy and full of crud. The food itself was good and the service in the dining room was par excellence (thanks to Doris, Ann, 'Arbo' the dishwasher, Jeff and the rest).

Nevertheless, I was having to pay a quarter of my salary for the honour of living in this decrepit place.

You have perhaps gathered by now, that I was not at all happy about being posted back to base camp!

By the time that we actually got down to it, task work itself was very enjoyable, in fact I would go as far as to say that by the time that we could start the task up to the time that the report had to be written, it was the best job in the Air Force. That middle bit was the bit that the officers left to us entirely.

It was a commonly held view that there were five distinct phases to any task that we did. These were:

1. Enthusiasm
2. Disillusionment
3. Panic as task completion date approaches

4. Search for the guilty
5. Praise and honour for the non-participants

I worked with a fine bunch of lads, mostly armourers, but also the flight included a couple of fairies and later on a couple of 'Rag Packers' (Safety Equippers who were sometimes also called 'squippers'), and we all seemed to get on pretty well.

I had kept my long-term tasks from Farnboro' and NATO Interoperability was still going strong. I still had a need to get to Germany at regular intervals, even though I had to have a paper fight to justify every trip.

Each of us in the flight would have our primary responsibilities and would be the nominated expert on the subject with which 'his chair' would be responsible for. For example, if someone was posted in to sit in the 'guns' chair, then that man became the 'RAF Expert' on guns, no matter what his previous experience had been. Common sense dictated of course that when someone was being interviewed for, say, the guns chair then we wanted someone who knew what he was talking about. The 'hands on' previous experience was a very important aspect of the job, even though the CSDE job itself was a completely different ball game.

I recall that at the beginning of one NATO Interop task, when a certain Wing Commander, one of the type who thinks that the RAF is merely a flying club, and should not be bothered by these tiresome weaponry type things, wrote in the file that he did not see any reason why I should go to Germany to gather information on how to prepare a publication for RAF personnel to modify and fit RAF weapons to a F104 Freedom Fighter of the German Air Force.

I really threw my teddy out of the cot.

Tact with the Officer Corps was never my best subject, maybe that was the reason why I was still a 'chief' after 15 years. Also perhaps it may have been after one of my Flight Commanders once wrote on my annual assessments that well-known quotation from the Holy Bible (Corinthians 11:19) 'Does not suffer fools gladly, especially when they are his superiors'.

I decided that I would write the publication on the information that I had got. I produced a front and back cover with a single page inside that read;

'Not known, unable to obtain information.'

My draft report, recommending task closure due to its completion, further recommended that the publication be distributed throughout all of the NATO headquarters staff (as was usual) for validation by the aircraft owner nation before subsequent use by the RAF.

The Wing Commander was not very pleased when I sent him the draft report, which also stated that the Wing Commander (he, himself, personally) had not felt any need for the specialist (me) to go to Germany to gather the appropriate information. I also included the Topic 12B-CL, which I did not normally do.

He suggested that I might like to pop over for a chat. I gave him a damn good listening to, but as I was never afraid of Wing Commanders, especially when they were like that one, who I considered to be a complete drain on the ration strength, I told him that the report stated the honest facts of the matter; the report was therefore incontrovertible. I told him that just because he was senior to me, did not necessarily mean that he was right. He didn't like that, not one jot. I asked him if he had ever seen an Interop Schedule, to which he gave the answer that I already knew.

'No.'

I told him that I would send him one, just so that he would get an idea of what was involved, and with that I then just walked out, I didn't even salute him.

He never gave me any trouble after that, but some of the other guys continued to have problems with him. He once wrote in somebody else's file that he had performed 'management on the hoof' just because he phoned somebody up. He had less idea on management than the hundreds of average Corporals who were running the 'tea bar' in every flight and squadron in the RAF.

There were a couple of other singlies in the flight. One, Alfie, lived in his own house in Sheringham and seemed to have his own life going on, and in any case we were not interested in the seaside with all those grockles (a Norfolk term of endearment (?) for tourists).

The other guy was Greig who lived 'in', like me. Greig and I would do the rounds of the clubs in Dereham and Norwich and before long we had both got ourselves entwined with a lady apiece. Greig and Margaret were getting on famously and so were Rita and I. In fact, Rita and I were getting on so well that one day I stood up in the flight to announce that this crinkly old chief was in love, and they were to keep their diaries clear for the wedding.

Yes, after ten years of freedom, I actually got married again and everyone from the flight attended.

A guy in the Flight called Simon Monks decided to research our patron saint. Now many people in the trade had always had suspicions that the armourers had a patron saint, but details were scant. Simon contacted the local vicar, who looked up in the book of saints to see what could be found. Sure enough, a lady by the name of St Barbara was found and the text goes:

The emblem of St Barbara

The story of St Barbara, as told in the Golden Legend, is that she was a maiden of great beauty whose father, Dioscurus, shut her up in a tower to discourage the attentions of various suitors.

On discovering that she had become a Christian, Dioscurus made to kill her, but she was miraculously transported out of his reach (probably by an amorous armourer). Dioscurus then denounced her to the authorities, who captured her and subjected her to great torture. She refused to renounce her faith (or betray her armourer lover??) whereupon her father was ordered to put her to death by fire.

This he duly did and he was immediately struck by lightning and reduced to ashes. From the ninth century her cultus became very widely spread; because of her father's fate she was invoked against danger by lightning, and by an extension of this idea she was later to become the patron saint of gunners, miners and armourers.

Her special emblem is the tower.

The date of her martyrdom is 4th December.

The time that the incident occurred is likely to be circa AD 235 in Rome.

Needless to say, 4 December of every year is now cause for great celebration amongst the armament tribe who gather together, usually at the exclusion of all non armourers, in local hostelries around the world, to imbibe themselves of copious amounts of alcohol in the symbolic gesture of washing away the pain that our patron lady suffered and the volume of beer being symbolic for the amount of liquid that would have been enough to put out the fire.

Our Swanton Morley settlement of the great Armourers' clan, used to gather in the 'Papermakers' pub in Swanton Morley village for a meal and a few jars.

Later on, when we started to invite affiliated armourers and retired armourers, the numbers of us were too many for The Papermakers to handle so we switched to the sports club on camp. This had a number of advantages in that we could all arrange accommodation in the old Nissen huts and we could run the bar ourselves. It was a simple 'automatic pilot' process to get us from the club to bed.

We also arranged the mandatory curry from the cookhouse to go with the beer. (If you are going to be sick you may as well bring up some solids as well to make it all worthwhile.) We actually used to make a small profit from this (shame! shame!) so we used that money to have a small 'couth' evening in The Papermakers at a later date, with our respective partners.

Long may this tradition of celebrating St Barbara's martydom be undertaken.

One day, a guy called Saddam Hussein decided that he wanted to be dictator of Kuwait as well as Iraq. He marched his men into Kuwait and took it over.

Now the whole of the Arab world has the policy that Arab can fight Arab with impunity. (Hence the War between Iran and Iraq that no-one took the slightest interest in.) This was a bit different though as the Kuwaitis had a protection treaty with the UK for years, and in any case, Saddam was getting too big for his boots and the rest of the Arab world was beginning to be afraid of him.

The rest is history.

As always under these conditions, the CSDE (especially the armourers and electricians), were running around like idiots ensuring that the things that the Air Force should have had years ago, were provided for the war. (Just like the Falklands really; will we ever learn?)

My part in this was interoperability, but this time the rules were a bit different. This time I only had to concentrate on the Jaguar and Tornado aircraft that were in theatre. The imagined scenario was that either of these aircraft could lob in to an American base and be re-armed with weapons of US manufacture.

The biggest problem was that the weapons had to be adapted and fitted to the aircraft by USAF personnel who had never before seen a Jag or Tonka, let alone worked on one.

Now the old interop schedule had more words and pictures than the usual schedules, but when a complete and utter stranger, a Yank to boot, is going to be let loose on your hairyplane with things that go 'bang', then those words and pictures have to be pretty accurate and simple. One of old Murphy's laws, 'If something can go wrong, it will', was uppermost in my mind.

All terminology had to be in Americanese for a start. I had my own copy of Webster's American Dictionary.

I wrote the first draft of the books as best I could. Nothing for it now but to try the proof of the pudding. This of course was to fly in one each of the aircraft to the USAFE base at Lakenheath, select a team of Yanks, who thought that the British Jaguar was a car, and another team who thought that Tornado was English for Hurricane, the strong wind variety.

We gave them the book and the kite (aircraft), stood aside and let them get on with it. They did pretty well.

I hoped that I had disproved another of Murphy's famous laws: 'When you explain something so carefully that no-one could possibly misunderstand, somebody will.' At least I hope that it had been disproved. If anything had gone wrong it would have been that particular Murphy's law that I would have quoted as my defence.

After the verification, the books were printed and rushed out to theatre in time for Desert Storm (I don't think that the British civilian populace ever knew that we called it 'Operation Granby').

I was then called upon to use my knowledge of foreign weapons to act as an advisor to the MoD. I was sent down to MoD PE (Procurement Executive) in London where, apart from anything else, I typed out the requisition for those Spanish Mk 82 500 lb bombs with the M1000 and M2000 fuzes. (Over six million pounds we paid for them!) Sorry lads, I know what problems you had with them later on!

It was during a trip down the corridor in PE that I overheard a conversation between my temporary Wing Commander and his Air Commodore.

'No!' thinks I. 'That's no good'.

When the Wing Commander was finally on his own I tackled him about what I had overheard. This was, in a nutshell, that four Hercules aircraft (Fat Alberts) would soon be on their way to Australia to pick up some kit for Tornado.

I briefed him that the kit that they were discussing would not be of any use for Tornado as it would not work. (I won't go into details, probably still classified.) This was about 1630 hrs on a Friday night and I was off to catch my train back to Norwich.

Whilst soaking in the bath at home that night, the phone rang and Rita answered it. She brought the phone in and this agitated officer from 'down the hole' in London was rabbiting on about four Fat Alberts being held up in Singapore because of what I had said. I repeated my reasoning to him and he said that the aircraft may as well turn round as the Aussies had nothing else on offer that would be of any use to us.

It was at that time that the doubts arose. Was I right or was I wrong? I suffered a bit that weekend I can tell you.

Come the Monday morn, I was called in to see the Air Commodore. I took the books (APs) in with me and proved to him that I had been right. Phew and phew again.

During Granby, we were using so many of our stock of 1000 lb bombs that we started to run out, and so we began to fit 500 lb bombs of various manufacture but to US design (the Mark 82).

Nations around the world were offering us Mk 82 gratis, plus lots of other kit up to 2000 lb LGB (Laser Guided Bomb) beasts (GBU 24 (Guided Bomb Unit) series). The Pussycats were already being fitted with CBU 87 (Cluster Bomb Unit) Gator and Canadian CRV 7 (Canadian Rocket Vehicle) rockets. Most of these funny weapons were already covered by the interop schedule. It was decided that someone had to travel the world and have a look at all this kit, just to make sure that it would be of use to us. Further, as I was the 'UK Expert' on foreign weapons, I was the chosen one. Me, a jet setter.

I seemed to spend the next week talking on the phone to British Embassies around the world and ended with a long list of countries to visit. The paperwork was started, and I had plane tickets in my hand to fly to South America, then to a European 'sunny' nation, then to a

Middle East destination, then to a far East destination and many more trips would be arranged by the time that I eventually got back. All accommodation would be arranged by the various British Embassies and cars and drivers laid on. I was looking forward to this.

The day before I was to make my first flight, Saddam capitulated. I have never been so disappointed in my life, I could have got used to being a jet setter.

The Air Force starred yet again and after only six months of married life I received the famous 'blue' letter offering me promotion. With it went a posting to Valley in Anglesey.

Anglesey is the place where the famous 'Valley walk' is practised. The Valley walk is where you walk at a permanent forty-five degree angle, due to the ever present, hundred mph wind.

Valley may as well have been at the other side of the world instead of just the other side of the country. Rita stated that there was no way that she would go to Valley and leave her beloved Norwich. The route between Anglesey and Norwich by both road and rail was an impossible journey, so I turned down my promotion.

After a year, I learned the true meaning of the saying 'There's no fool like an old fool' and realised that I had made a ginormous (a combination of 'gigantic' and 'enormous', and more correctly called a 'portmanteau word' – bet you didn't know that!) mistake.

My new wife had some pretty rigid ideas of what married life was supposed to be all about. This included voicing her opinion that 'everybody takes their wives into Norwich every Saturday afternoon so that they (the wives) can go into every dress shop and feel the material of every dress in the shop, even the very same dresses that were felt last week', and 'Everybody goes out on a Saturday night', and 'Everybody gets in their cars and drives around in a big circle getting nowhere on a Sunday afternoon', and 'Everybody goes down to the beach on a public holiday'.

No way Jose, after less than two years of married life we got divorced.

There is no one woman in the world who has all the best points of every woman that I have ever known combined together. If such a person ever did exist it would be a different story, but such a person could never exist.

Just before I had married, I had even written to Jennie in Germany to tell her about my impending troth. I never heard from her again so I had burned my bridges there. Even though I continued to go to Germany

176

many times after the divorce, I did not attempt to see Jennie again. I felt that I should not open up any old wounds.

Greig's lady-friend introduced me to one of her pals and we got on well. We got on even better when she, Norma, told me that there was no way that she wanted to get involved with a man again, just companionship and sex was all that she wanted.

Good oh! She was obviously a girl after my own heart.

Later, she changed her mind and said that she did want someone on a more permanent basis. Yes, she was a girl after my own heart alright, but not in the way that I had first thought.

'Oh well, that's life', as Ned Kelly, the famous Australian outlaw said just before they hanged him in 1880.

The trouble with you, girls, is that you fall in love with us fellers far too easily. It does have some definite advantages from our point of view but it also has a down side.

After the divorce I decided that I would never get involved with another woman no matter what the circumstances were. I would not even live with one, be it my house or her house; from now on I was destined to be a self confessed and dedicated professional singlie.

I decided that I needed some sort of physical project to divert my energies away from 'bad news' women. One of my lifetime ambitions had been to either build my own house or convert a barn to residential use, and right at that point in time seemed to be the ideal opportunity. Anyway, I was not getting any younger, and decided that if I did not make a start PDQ (Pretty Damn Quick), then I would never achieve that ambition.

I bought a barn.

I decided that I would do everything myself, or at least 99% of it. I made my initial sketches and took them to Sketchers (an appropriate name for a house design company), and after planning permission got underway, so did I. I bought a little old caravan and put it inside the barn and moved out of the mess. It was a bit basic but what the heck, I had been expected to live in far worse conditions than this in the service of my country so I could certainly tolerate this for a while. It was hard work but it was fun and very satisfying.

I started chatting with my next-door neighbour over the garden fence and it transpired that she was a divorcee with a fifteen year old daughter.

I gave her a bottle of beer sometimes and she gave me a cup of tea sometimes.

* * *

As I have said before, the 'hands on' work at CSDE is great. It is the niff-naff and trivia that spoils it. The CSDE was full of snecks with hardly a junior rank in sight, so when the guard roster was started, compliments of the IRA, the guard post was manned by Chief Technicians and Sergeants, instead of the usual SAC, JT and Corporals. Yes, we were still getting paid lots of money, but it meant that we were away from work for over a week. Now that is not what I call VFM (Value For Money).

A concrete guard post was eventually installed for our protection. Now this concrete guard post was nicknamed 'Concrete Condom', by virtue of the fact that it ensheathed all of our vulnerable parts and protected the 'wearer' from unwanted mishaps. Sitting in the condom with a rifle and real bullets to play with was boring in the extreme, and once all the jokes had been read there was not a lot to do except to sit and look at every person, bird, rat, slug and leaf that moved.

Sometimes, to break the monotony of the night shift, someone actually came to the gate and we would have to radio the policeman in the shed on the other side of the road to wake him up or to have a break from bonking his girlfriend so that he could go and let them in. The morning shift, when everyone came in to work in their hundreds, if not thousands, was a veritable feast of excitement. What a sad lot we were! Some of the jokes written on the condom wall were pretty good though (at least in my opinion), and I include a few:

Anoraknaphobia – The fear of overcoats.
Anuraknaphobia – The fear of Indian restaurants.
Awracnaphobia - The fear of army girls.
Did you hear about the dyslexic muslim who tried to kill Willie Rushton?
Does a supervisor help you see better?
   Caesar adsum jam forte
   Brutus aderat
   Caesar sic in omnibus
   Brutus inisat
Condom definition – Periods of great inactivity followed by periods of extreme boredom.
Why is there just one monopolies commission?
Did you hear about the Dyslexic atheist insomniac – He lay awake all night wondering if there was a dog.
TGIF – Thank God it's Fursday (Thursday was guard change day after the week's shift).

Life is a book, in here, is just a sentence.

If I had a penny for each two-hour stint I had been in here, I would have £3 and 27p by now. (Obviously an old timer like me)!

Is this what a baked bean feels like?

Apart from the guarding aspect and the nauseating paperwork that I have already mentioned, another greatly annoying aspect of the CSDE was the report writing. As everyone knows, there is more than one way to skin a cat and more than one way to write a sentence. Not as far as the Officer Corps are concerned. Even mail incoming to the unit would first have its English corrected by one of the hierarchy who would be reading it first, that is how pathetic they were. Any report that we had to produce was first done in draft, which would then be given to our line managers who would re-write it and pass it on to his line manager, who would re-write it and pass it on to his line manager, ad infinitum ad nausea. The end result was that the report ended up by never saying what we wanted it to say in the first place, and anything that was in the remotest bit contentious would be deleted.

A typical example would be during a fictitious report on mice where the report states:

Mice have four feet.

Management comment: Elaborate!

Revision 1: Mice have five appendages of which four are feet.

Management comment: No discussion on fifth appendage!

Revision 2: Mice have five appendages, of which four are feet with the remaining one being a tail.

Management comment: What, feet with no legs?

Revision 3: Mice have four legs, four feet, and one tail per unit mouse.

Management comment: Confusing – is that a total of nine appendages?

Revision 4: Mice have four leg/foot assemblies and one tail assembly per body.

Management comment: Does not fully discuss the issue!

Revision 5: Each mouse comes equipped with four legs and a single tail. Each leg is equipped with a foot at the opposite end from the body. However, the tail is not equipped with a foot.

Management comment: Descriptive – yes, forceful – no!

Revision 6: Allocation of appendages for mice will be four leg/foot assemblies and one tail. Deviation from this policy is not permitted, as it would constitute misuse of scarce appendage assets.

Management comment: Too authoritarian, stifles creativity!

Revision 7: Mice have four feet, each of which is attached to a small leg which itself is joined integrally with the overall mouse structural system. Also attached to the mouse system is a thin tail, which is non-functional and ornamental in nature.

Management comment: Too verbose and scientific, just answer the question!

Final revision approved a week later by management: Mice have four feet.

I remember a report that I drafted once on future weapon storage. The subject was a contentious one admittedly. However, the report was changed so much that I washed my hands of it and removed my name from the bottom where it said 'Investigating SNCO'.

The report was finally sent off to the MoD.

After a few days, the Wing Commander from the ministry rang me up and asked what the report was all about. I pointed out that I had removed my name from the bottom, which he said he had noted. I told him that I still had my original draft and if he wanted me to, I would send him a copy. He said, 'bring it down'. This I did, and he and the Group Captain read it together and said, 'Now we can see what it is all about.' With that they ripped out the 'official' report from the file, threw it in the 'confidential waste' bin and inserted my draft in the file.

All that time, wasted by the CSDE Officer Corps. Power games and smarty points is all that they were interested in.

CSDE reports, reminds me of a joke:

Two men in a balloon flew into mist and were completely lost. They decided to sink slowly to the ground and drift around until they saw someone that they could ask. This they eventually did and shouted down to the fellow 'Ahoy there, we are lost. Could you please tell us where we are exactly?'

The voice comes back from the man below 'You are in a balloon'.

'Thank you' shouts the man in the balloon, who immediately gets out his maps and shows his companion their location.

'But how do you know where we are?' asks his companion.

'Because that man gave us an entirely accurate but entirely useless answer. Therefore he has to be an officer from the CSDE at RAF Swanton Morley.'

They were right you know, and they found their way home.

Neighbour's daughter passes NINE GCSEs, eight at A STAR level and one at A level. Bright girl!

Neighbour asks if she can look after my garden as she loves gardening. 'Of course,' says I, who hate gardening. I give her a pretty basic plan and off she goes and does all the digging, planting and tending. She loves digging, mowing the grass and especially, weeding! Great!

Due to my involvement with foreign weapons, I was asked if I would be a one man Project Team for SR(A) 1242 (Staff Requirement (Air) number 1242), this is where the operators (the fly-boys) say that they want a particular piece of kit to do a job. In this case it was for an armour-piercing guided weapon.

All the usual RFIs (Request For Information) were sent out, then tenders requested from about twelve companies around the world. Three responded.

Two of the companies provided their tenders bound in fancy books of about ten volumes each. One French company returned their tender, metaphorically, scribbled on the back of a fag packet. (Is this the way that the French do business?)

Amazing really, as £400 million had been allotted for this contract.

Tender assessment and pre-contract negotiations followed, and I did my bit for ILS and LSA (Integrated Logistic Support and Logistic Support Analysis). The contract was awarded to Texas Instruments of Sherman, Texas for the supply of Paveway III(UK) with a 2000 lb penetrator warhead.

'Jolly jolly,' thinks I, knowing that the Project Team (called the LLLGBPT viz Low Level Laser Guided Bomb Project Team) of just one person i.e. ME, would be based at the company. 'Texas here I come.' Little did I realise that Texas Instruments had a factory in Bedford, in 'l'il ole England'. Damn!

By this time the Berlin wall was being sold brick by brick to tourists and the Air Force was going to have to undergo a mighty change, due to the fact that all of a sudden, we were mostly out of a job. Part of the changes involved the closure of RAF Swanton Morley with a move of its inhabitants to RAF Wyton, which was going to be the new headquarters of the all singing, all dancing RAF Support Command. Massive redundancies were rumoured and morale in the Air Force sank to an all time low.

At this time I had been tasked with writing the document for an office review. This was a paper to justify the existence of the flight and the number of personnel in it. The boss was away and my job on the Project Team (not yet moved to Bedford), was not using all of my time. Everybody else in the flight was busy with the Bosnia thing, and the

181

Flight Sergeant was on his EOD/IED (Explosive Ordnance Disposal/ Improvised Explosive Devices) course so, as the senior 'chief', the job was mine.

The Squadron Leader stated that the document was to pull no punches. Great! just the 'licence to kill' that I liked. I wrote a few home truths, including the fact that morale was so bad, due to the fact that the 'powers that be' (another biblical expression; Romans 13:1) were not disseminating any information on redundancies or the impending move to Wyton.

My Wing Commander actually came over to see me and we had a heart to heart in the hangar. He said that little information was being passed from the 'powers that be' and he saw no reason why he should pass on the scant information that he had. He rocked on his heels when I informed him that as far as we were concerned, the 'powers that be' started with him. That simple fact had never dawned on him.

Further discussion on manpower establishment gave him another setback on his heels, when I expounded one of my own laws to him in that 'Those who have least work to do, have most time to justify their existence'. Another simple fact that had never occurred to him!

When the Project Team was officially formed, I went off to be based at Wyton as the very first CSDE man there, but it was only for accommodation purposes, as I was commuting daily to Bedford to my little office at TI (Texas Instruments).

I would then drive home to my barn at weekends for a bit of strenuous exercise by continuing with the conversion. (I was still using a ladder to get to bed at this time, not the best of aids for my seduction technique.)

Next-door neighbour's daughter had now passed three 'A' levels at grade A and next-door neighbour was feeding me and giving me massages to ease my weary body (she was a qualified masseuse).

She would also dig the trench for the foundations of my new garage and workshop whilst I was away during the week. All that I had to do was to lay the string line and tell her how deep to dig: the 'technical bit' as she used to say.

I'm glad my neighbour likes digging!

Before the first of the bulk of the CSDE guys were due to move to Wyton, TI decided that they were to close down their factory in Bedford and move the salesmen, ASIC (Application Specific Integrated Circuit) and MOS (Metal Oxide Semi-conductors) design teams, along with the Defence Systems guys to Northampton.

This of course included me and I found myself on lodging allowance again.

I was commuting back to my barn in Bawdeswell, and by now my next door neighbour had decided that she would clean up the barn and generally look after me.

She had very old fashioned ideas that it is a woman's job to do everything in the house, a woman does all the cooking, a woman carries all the shopping bags and things like that.

This, on top of the massages every night!

Time passes on and the Air Force decide to have a first tranche of redundancies. Not a single armourer is included on the list. When the second tranche of redundancies is announced, it includes armourers and the redundancy exit date would coincide nicely with my job on the Project Team coming to an end. At the end of my Project Team Job it had been planned that I would go back to Wyton for the last 18 months of my service career. Back to wearing a uniform and all the nausea of things like duties and guards and horrible un-necessary paperwork etc.

I applied for redundancy and was successful. My Wing Commander rang me up and said that he was very surprised that I had even applied! After 38 years in the RAF, they would give me just over £4000 in redundancy money; generous or what!

I took all the resettlement courses that I was entitled to, including the 'spoof' ones that had been set up for redundees. These were summarised thus:

A new scheme will be introduced for redundees and for people who would be taking early retirement. This scheme has been given the acronym RAPE (Retired Airman, Personnel, Early). Personnel selected to be RAPED, may apply to management for eligibility for the SHAFT (Special Help AFTerwards) scheme. Personnel who have been RAPED and SHAFTED will, at a later date, be reviewed under the SCREW (Special Chances for Retired Early Workers) scheme. Personnel may be RAPED only once, SHAFTED a maximum of three times but SCREWED as many times as necessary.

Personnel who have already been RAPED, may apply to get AIDS (Additional Income for Dependents or Spouses) or HERPES (Half Earnings for Retired Personnel on Early Severance). However, personnel who have AIDS or HERPES are to be aware that they are unlikely to be SHAFTED or SCREWED by management in the future.

Note; Personnel who do not elect to retire, will, in the future, expect to receive as much SHIT (Special High Intensity Training) as possible. The service has always prided itself on the amount of SHIT it has been able to give personnel in the past but we can assure you that you will receive very much more SHIT in the future.

I looked back at my 15 years in total at the CSDE, and reckon that I had travelled to Germany (which then may have involved further trips into Holland, Belgium, France or Denmark) thirty-nine times, Stockholm, four times, Texas, three times and MoD in London, factories and bases in this country hundreds of times, all on the Queen's business.

I also looked back at my 38 years in the RAF and came to the conclusion that too many people are performing the management function (especially officers but also a few SNCOs). I have my own law that would explain this:

> The whole purpose of management is to make an organisation so efficient, that management would no longer be required.

What this would have meant, was that efficient management would work themselves out of a job, and that they would never do.

I did the circuit with my 'blue card' for the very last time.

They took away my RAF Form 1250 (Identity Card) and it was manumission time, I was a civilian.

RETIREMENT IN NORFOLK

(Society of Ex RAF Personnel – (SERPs))
(Recognisable by the person wearing an RAF shirt)

I had been psyching myself up for retirement for a long time, and it eventually arrived. I applied for a disability pension and was judged to be 20% disabled so I am now classed as a war pensioner. This adds just over £22 pounds per week tax free to my pension, so that makes up for not retiring as a Warrant Officer. I look back at the fifteen units that I have been posted to and find that ten of them have now closed down. I spent 10 years at RAF Swanton Morley and fifteen years continuous at the CSDE, so I suppose that I did decide that I liked it in the end. Prior to that I had never spent more than three years in any one posting, so for me it was a bit of a record.

The number of what I would call 'good' officers that I have known in my life, I can count on one hand, perhaps with a couple of fingers on the other hand. The rest I do not consider worth the money that the taxpayer gives them. I would also say that something like 50% of SNCOs are worth their salt but even then, most of that 50% are worth more to the country than the country pays them.

The barn is now completely finished, as is the second house that I built from foundations up and found to be a very profitable venture. I then bought a 250-year-old house, extended and modernised it over a three year period.

At the age of 65, I now drive a Mazda MX5 sports car and am about to start driving my 47-year-old BMW Isetta bubble car, once I have sorted out the wheel bearings.

Do I regret my life? Not one second of it.

Would I do it again? Not if I knew what I know now, but Yes, if I was a young lad.

My next-door neighbour's daughter has now left university after passing her BSc. (Hons) and works at an education facility in the Norfolk Broads. Did I marry my next-door neighbour, I hear you ask.

You don't think I'm stupid do you? Of course I did. She exhibits every good point of every woman that I have ever known and more besides.

I will finish this off with the words of the Armourers' anthem, which pleases non-armourers, as they all seem to make comment about our intelligence, and it was produced as a tongue-in-cheek sop to the other trades. However, we armourers know the truth. The truth being that we armourers are the greatest folk who ever existed on this planet, especially those of us who started out their lives in the 91st Entry, at good old RAF Halton.

The Armourers' Anthem

(This song should be sung to the, by now rather old fashioned, song that went – A – You're adorable, B – You're so beautiful, etc.)

A – I'm an Armourer
B – I'm an Armourer
C – I'm an Armourer as well
D – I'm an Armourer
E – I'm an Armourer
F – and the rest can go to hell
G – I'm an Armourer
H – I'm an Armourer
I am an Arm-or-rer
J – I'm an Armourer
K – I'm an Armourer
L – I'm an 'ell of a guy
M – I'm an Armourer
O – I'm an Armourer
P – I'm the Prince of the sky
Q – I'm an Armourer
R – I'm an Armourer
S – I'm the Saviour of the land
T – I'm an Armourer
U – I'm an Armourer
V – I'm the Victor in the sand
W – I'm an Armourer
X – I'm an Armourer
YZ – (wise) I'm the wisest cos I'm an ARM-OR-RER.